Beating
Wife-Beating

Beating Wife-Beating

Lee H. Bowker
Indiana University
of Pennsylvania

LexingtonBooks
D.C. Heath and Company
Lexington, Massachusetts
Toronto

Library of Congress Cataloging in Publication Data

Bowker, Lee Harrington.
  Beating wife-beating.

  Includes index.
  1. Abused wives—Wisconsin—Milwaukee—Attitudes—Case studies.
2. Wife abuse—Wisconsin—Milwaukee—Case studies. 3. Family violence—
Wisconsin—Milwaukee—Case studies. 4. Abused wives—Services for—
Wisconsin—Milwaukee—Case studies. I. Title.
HV6626.B68 1983   362.8'3   82-48603
  ISBN 0-669-06345-2

Second printing, February 1984

Published simultaneously in Canada

Printed in the United States of America

International Standard Book Number: 0-669-06345-2

Library of Congress Catalog Card Number: 82-48603

Contents

Figures and Tables

Acknowledgments

I would like to express my appreciation to the staff of the Milwaukee project. They did an excellent job under difficult conditions, as the complexity of the research, and, therefore, the workload, continually expanded beyond our expectations. Special thanks are due to Kristine MacCallum, who conducted the interviews and contributed to the project in many other ways; to Thomas Callan, who was responsible for data processing; and to MaryAnn Riggs, who produced this and other project manuscripts. Professors William Feyerherm, Audrey Smith, and Elam Nunnally were generous with advice and support throughout the project, as were James Breiling and Tom Lally at the National Institute of Mental Health. Pat Flannery, who supervises the Research Support Office of the Center for Advanced Studies in Human Services, and many of her staff members worked overtime to complete the data processing on a tight schedule. The research on which this book is based was carried out under Grant #1 RO1 MH33649 from the National Institute of Mental Health.

Beating
Wife-Beating

1 A Brief Examination of the Literature

Wife-beating has always been with us. Goode [1] goes so far as to argue that the family, like all social units, rests to some degree on the threat or use of force. Dobash and Dobash [2] and Martin [3, 4] are among those who have assembled historical material to show that wife-beating has been common throughout the ages. In fact, a man's responsibility as a good citizen was at one time considered to include giving his wife both verbal instructions on how to live her life and beatings as often as necessary to help her follow his instructions to the letter.

It seems likely that wife-beating in the contemporary United States differs from the historical phenomenon in two fundamental ways. First, wife-beating is probably less common today than it was during earlier historical periods. Second, although wife-beating may be gradually declining in frequency, it has come to be seen as a social problem. Many of the social devices used to oppress women have been removed, and they have been granted the right to own property, the right to vote, and so forth. As these structural changes in society were taking place, there was a parallel change in the amount of physical violence that was considered legitimate for a husband to use against his wife. Women could not be first-class citizens and still be beaten senseless by their husbands. The most recent step in this process was the rise of the women's movement, which has been associated with increases in the public concern about wife-beating, the variety and extensiveness of services provided to the victims of wife-beating, and the number and quality of scholarly studies on the subject.

In the days when wife-beating was not considered to be a social problem, nobody ever thought to keep records of the practice. When social scientists, practitioners, and movement activists began the task of collecting and publishing information on wife-beating, there were no standard guidelines. Therefore, the literature that has emerged contains a wide variety of methodologies for obtaining data about wife-beating. In the past decade, statistics on wife-beating have been collected from police and court records, and from the files of shelters for battered women and other social-service agencies. Several investigators have made use of groups of couples who were identified at the point at which they applied for divorce. Student groups have been sampled in some studies, and other investigations have used haphazard samples of adults. More recently, the biases that are inherent in these methods of subject identification and selection have been avoided by draw-

1

ing random samples, both locally and nationally. The contributions made by these studies are briefly noted in the following sections.

Agency and Official Statistics

Dobash and Dobash [5] found that 34 percent of all of the violent offenses reported to police departments in Edinburgh and Glasgow, Scotland in 1974 were assaults between family members. Most of these domestic assaults (76 percent) were committed against wives by their husbands, while only 1 percent were committed against husbands by wives. The pattern of males attacking females was also prevalent in other family assaults, such as assaults of parents by children, of children by parents, and between siblings [6].

Statistics from police departments show a high degree of variability, as one might expect from the divergence in their departmental policies about accepting and recording family-assault complaints. When only a small proportion of the domestic assaults that are reported to the police are recorded as crimes [7, 8], the effect of departmental policies is magnified, and even a mandatory battered-spouse reporting law cannot eliminate this problem [9]. For example, in the Washtenaw, Michigan County Sheriff's Department, 50 percent of all assault and battery complaints were found to have been filed by women against their husbands. In a Montgomery County, Maryland study, one in every thirteen calls to police regarding domestic problems involved physical assault against wives by husbands. Thirty-two percent of all the aggravated assaults identified in a search of Kansas City police files were domestic [10]. Data from a sample of police chiefs in Wisconsin were used to estimate an average of 54 cases of domestic violence per 10,000 citizens. Alcohol or drugs were involved in 70 percent of these incidents [11], but in only 30 to 56 percent of a sample of cases from a different area studied by Bard and Zacker [12].

Court statistics can also be used as an indication of the extent of domestic violence, although these statistics underestimate the actual incidence of domestic violence even more than police reports. In New York City, the number of new petitions in the family court charging a family offense rose from 4,803 in 1974 to 7,237 in 1975 [13]. One hundred court cases involving marital violence in a Canadian city were observed by Whitehurst [14] and his students. In nearly all of these cases, the husbands attacked their wives out of frustration because they were unable to control them as completely as they wished. Although O'Brien [15] did not ask directly about family violence, one-sixth of his interviewees (all of whom had initiated a divorce action) spontaneously mentioned violence. Levinger [16] found that 37 percent of a sample of 600 couples applying for divorce involved the physical abuse of wives, while only three percent included the physical abuse of husbands. The number of alleged incidents of family violence reported to district attorneys in Wisconsin was estimated to be nearly 6,000 in 1976, for a rate of 12.1 per 10,000 citizens. [11].

Statistics can also be collected from a variety of social-service agencies, such as the legal-aid office. Forty-two percent of fifty consecutive females asking for help from the Domestic Relations Division of the Baltimore Legal Aid Bureau were found to have been victims of wife-beating, which generalized to approximately one thousand cases per year at the central office of this agency. [17].

During a fifteen month period, six hundred female clients were seen by the Brooklyn Legal Services Corporation, of which 60 percent admitted having been beaten during their marriage. The proportion of white clients who had been beaten (71 percent) was considerably higher than the proportion of blacks (59 percent) or Puerto Ricans (54 percent). Fields [18] also found that when beaten women were compared with other women served by the agency, they were younger, better educated, and more likely to have been pregnant within one year prior to or after their marriages. Smaller samples of women receiving help from social-service agencies were used by Pfouts [19] and Ball [20] to develop theories about wife-beating.

Gayford [21, 22, 23] studied one hundred battered wives at a women's aid hostel, a technique that was also used by Carlson [24], Rounsaville [25], Pagelow [26, 27], Ferraro [28, 29], Frieze and her associates [30, 31, 32], Browne [33], McNeely and Jones [34], Reynolds [35], the URSA Institute [36], Vaughan [37], LaBell [38], Korlath [39], Star [40], and Dobash and Dobash [2, 41, 42]. These studies concentrated on the worst of the wife-beating cases. Many of them produced moving stories of continuous abuse stretching over many years, and detailed descriptions of the physical and emotional injuries suffered by the victims. In a recent report from a shelter for abused women, Ashley [43] indicates that more than four-fifths of the women seeking aid at a San Francisco shelter had children and about 40 percent of them had previously been the victims of violence in their parents' homes.

Pagelow [27] mainly used volunteers from Florida and California battered-women's shelters to make-up her sample of 350 beaten wives. A quarter of her respondents reported physically fighting back when attacked by their husbands or partners, despite an average weight disadvantage of forty-four pounds. Only 28 percent of the women had observed their mothers being beaten by their fathers, as compared with 53 percent of the aggressors having observed such violence. A total of 155 out of the 350 women approached law agencies for help, as compared with 99 who approached psychiatrists or psychologists, 78 who approached the clergy, and 51 who approached marriage counselors.

Frieze differs from the previously named researchers in that she included a comparison group of unbeaten volunteer women to match the women recruited from shelters via posted advertisements or from public records identifying those who had filed against their husbands on the Pennsylvania Protection from Abuse Act. It is interesting that 48 of the 137 comparison group volunteers (35 percent) had to be segregated into a third group, designated control battered, because they were also the victims of marital violence. Many of the battered women in the original sample had suffered violence while pregnant (52 percent) or marital rape (34 percent). The most common help-sources utilized by those women were relatives (55 percent), friends (52 percent), social-service agencies (43 percent), therapists (42 percent), and priests (39 percent) [32]. Women who blamed themselves for the violence were less likely than the other victims to physically fight back to seek help from friends and relatives, but were more likely to seek help from therapists [31]. In a preliminary study using a reduced sample, Frieze [30] found that violent couples used more negative power strategies than nonviolent couples and that violence was used by husbands as part of their strategy to increase power over their wives.

Another way to use agency statistics is to survey agencies rather than individuals within an agency. Using this technique, Spezeski and Warner [44] found that only 16 percent of agency representatives in San Diego County rated spouse abuse as a serious community problem, and just 18 percent saw a need for emergency shelters for the victims of spouse abuse. A survey of 163 programs providing services to battered women by Back et al. [45] found that 73 percent of the women served were white, 44 percent had been battered by husbands or partners having semiskilled or unskilled occupations, and 32 percent had been battered by aggressors having at least some college education. Roberts [46] found that just over half of his national sample of shelters had been in existence for less than a year. From his findings, he estimated that over 100,000 women seek help from crisis hotlines and shelters each year. Questionnaires returned by twelve community organizations serving battered women in Wisconsin identified a total of 1,618 contacts during 1977, of which 1,000 were in Milwaukee, 200 in Madison, 165 in Kenosha, and 90 in Racine. Twenty percent of these contacts involved shelter care and 84 percent involved counseling the victims [11].

Studies of Groups from the General Population

If one wants to know how serious wife-beating can be, interviewing shelter-care residents and other specialized populations of victims is an appropriate technique. If, on the other hand, one wants to know something about wife-beating in the general population, it is necessary to draw samples from other sources. One strategy that has been used on several occasions is to administer questionnaires to samples of students. Whitehurst [14] distributed questionnaires to students in three of his classes in a study of male sexual aggressiveness. Adler [47] conducted in-depth interviews with a sample of 50 couples, which comprised all of the married part-time graduate students at a New England state college. Using this technique, Adler was able to show how marital power and the use of violence are related to each other. In an innovative study, Straus [48] asked students in introductory sociology and anthropology courses to complete a questionnaire about conflict in their families during the last year they were in high school. He found that the expression of verbal aggression was directly related to physical aggression, rather than inversely related, which is inconsistent with the leveling, catharsis, and ventilation theories of aggression. A later report on these data [49] supports the idea that wife-beating is often used by husbands as the ultimate support to their claim of power entitlement when other resources are not sufficient.

Unselected or volunteer samples derived from the population at large may be more representative of the general population than samples of students. Although volunteer samples have only recently been used in studies of family violence, they have been used for many years in investigations of other sensitive subjects. Kinsey and his associates [50] carried out their research on human sexual behavior using volunteer subjects, and this tradition has been continued in recent national studies of female sexuality [51], group sex [52], and lesbianism [53, 54]. Two of the first volunteer studies of wife-beating were carried out by Gelles [55, 56, 57, 58] and Marsden and Owens [59]. Marsden and Owens advertised for volunteers in a small town in the United Kingdom, obtaining 19 volunteers in this fashion. Even with a sample of this size, they identified multiple violence patterns and concluded that wife-beating is such a complex phenomenon that it cannot be explained by any single theory or model. *The Violent Home*, by Gelles [55], presents the data obtained in interviews with eighty families. Included among his conclusions are that (1) a marriage license often functions as a hitting license, (2) many wives are beaten while they are pregnant, and (3) there are a number of systematic factors related to whether or not a beaten wife will leave her husband.

Volunteers have been used as subjects in recent studies by Whitehurst [60], Billings et al. [61], Adrian and Mitchell [62], Doran [63], Frieze, McCreanor and Shomo [64], and in the ongoing research program conducted by Walker [65, 66, 67, 68]. Walker used 120 case histories contributed by battered women to develop a three-stage model of wife-beating that is one of the most significant theoretical advances in the understanding of family violence. The three stages are (1) the slow, tense escalation of violence, (2) an explosion of relatively severe battering, and (3) the reconciliation, in which the aggressor seduces his mate into continuing the relationship, following which the cycle repeats itself. A questionnaire by Doron was printed in a New Jersey newspaper, drawing 612 responses and 180 interview volunteers. Forty-three of these women had been the victims of marital rape. Frieze et al. report data from two small studies of men to show that female interviewers using careful probing and self-disclosure can be successful in obtaining marital-violence data from male subjects.

Random samples drawn from the normal population were not used in studies of wife-beating until the late 1970s. A small random sample drawn from New Castle County, Delaware was used by Steinmetz [69, 70, 71, 72]; a national survey of family violence was conducted by Straus, Gelles, and Steinmetz [73, 74, 75, 76, 77, 78, 79, 80, 81, 82, 83]; reanalyses of data from the National Crime Survey Program were completed by Gaquin [84] and by Saltzman and Featherston [85]; and other survey data were analyzed by Nisonoff and Bitmann [86], Ulbrich and Huber [87], Stachura and Teske [88] and Schulman [89].

Steinmetz found that 51 percent of the families she studied sometimes resolved marital conflicts by throwing things at each other, 31 percent by pushing, shoving, or grabbing, 22 percent by hitting spouses with their hands, and 12 percent by hitting spouses with something hard. There was a considerable similarity between husbands and wives in the types of aggression used and the frequency of use, but husbands inflicted more physical damage than did wives.

Gaquin's [84] secondary analysis of data from the National Crime Survey found that there were more than one million incidents of spouse abuse in the United States from 1973 through 1975. Approximately fifteen out of every one hundred assaults suffered by women in the United States during these years were perpetrated by their husbands or ex-husbands. However, this percentage is misleading because it includes many women who were never married. For women who were ever married, spouse abuse constituted 25 percent of all assaults. It was also responsible for 28 percent of the assaults on divorced women and an incredible 55 percent of all assaults on separated women. Spouse abuse was more likely than nonspousal assaults on women to involve an actual physical attack, to be judged to be a serious assault on the victim, to cause physical injury, and to require hospital treatment or other medical care.

A national study by Straus, Gelles, and Steinmetz [82] provides us with more details on wife-beating than most of these earlier studies. Marital violence occurred during 1975 for 16 percent of the couples interviewed and had occurred in the past for 28 percent of the couples. Husbands were only slightly more likely to use violence against wives than vice versa, but were considerably more likely to have seriously beaten up their spouses or to have used a knife or gun on them. Some of the respondents in the national survey were unmarried cohabitors, which allowed Yllo and Straus [73] to compare them to the married couples. Cohabitors in general were found to be considerably more violent than married couples, with a male to female overall violence-rate nearly three times the married rate. However, co-habitors who were over thirty years old, divorced women, those who had been living together for over ten years, and those with high incomes had very low rates of violence. In view of common stereotypes linking blacks to family violence, it is important to emphasize that black family violence was found to be less common than white family violence in this national study [74].

These studies establish two points about wife-beating. The first, which derives largely from clinical studies and from studies of other specialized populations, is that the experience of wife-beating is extremely damaging for the women. The seriousness, frequency, and unpredictability of incidents of abuse for these women is a major social problem. In addition, there is more than a little evidence [43, 81, 90, 91, 92] that wife-beating is also related to physical abuse of children. The second point is that wife-beating is a common occurrence in the United States, not an unusual or highly deviant act. In general, the literature suggests that the incidence of wife-beating rises drastically as the level of severity of acts committed against the wives decreases. That is to say, most of the wife-beating that occurs in the United States produces physical damage of low severity.

The Relationship between Wife-Beating and Marital Power

The severity and extensiveness of wife-beating are both important reasons to study its cessation, but there is a third reason that is also of great importance: wife-beating (even when it involves a very low level of violence, or perhaps only the threat of violence) has consequences for the balance of power in U.S. families. These power-balance consequences extend to a much wider range of families than we would expect from the figures on the national incidence of overt family-violence developed by Gaquin and by Straus, Gelles, and Steinmetz. To the extent that wife-beating diminishes a wife's freedom to contribute equally to decision-making processes in her family, it is morally unacceptable in a society that values individualism and democracy. It may also have negative consequences for her mental health and for the way in which she deals with her children. Taken together, the hypothesized relationships between wife-beating and (1) the marital balance of power, (2) mental health and (3) child abuse constitute a third complex of factors that necessitates a careful study of the cessation of wife-beating.

What does the literature on family power say about the relationship between decision-making dominance and wife-beating? Straus [93] found a link between family power and family violence in his analysis of data that college students reported about their parents. In a later paper on this survey, Allen and Straus [49] found that there was little or no relationship between the conjugal balance of power and the use of violence by either spouse. This was hypothesized to be because the husband would only resort to violence if his relative power in the family was lower than the level he could tolerate. However, relying on students' reports of their parents' behavior is dangerous. Students are not privy to many of the interactions that occur between their parents and may be poor judges of who wields the power in the family.

Dobash and Dobash [2] found remarkable and consistent patterns in the events leading up to wife-beating that were reported by 109 Scottish women, most of whom had sought refuge in houses for battered women. Many of the beatings occurred as a result of disagreements over minor domestic affairs. Any challenge made to the husband's authority in these minor areas greatly increased the chances of being beaten. In the families studied by Dobash and Dobash, the husband labelled any lengthy discussion or debate as nagging, which he saw as provoking and justifying his violent response.

Evidence about the relationship between marital power and wife-beating taken from severely beaten wives is unlikely to be representative of this relationship in the general population. However, there is one study that deals with the topic directly. This is "The Underside of Married Life: Power, Influence and Violence" by Emily Adler [47]. Adler studied fifty couples, at least one member of whom was a part-time graduate student. Thirty-four percent of the husbands and 32 percent of the wives had used violence against their spouses during their marriage, including hitting, pushing, kicking, and puching. Although the incidence of violence was similar for husbands and wives, the definitions of the violence differed. In 38 percent of assaults on husbands by wives, the husbands defined it as ineffective, nonthreatening, amusing, or annoying. None of the assaulted wives defined the situation in this way.

In Adler's sample, husbands were physically larger than wives in forty-eight of fifty cases. All but one of the husbands and two of the wives agreed that the husband was physically stronger than his mate. Except when dangerous weapons were used, which happened with only one of the wives in the study, the husbands were physically capable of controlling their wives by force. As a test of the relationship between the use of violence and control of the marriage, Adler correlated the use of violence with degree of domination, first by husbands and then wives. The use of violence by wives was essentially unrelated to the balance of power between the husbands and wives (Yule's Q=.09), but the use of violence by husbands was strongly associated with their dominance over their wives (Yule's Q=.53). Adler concluded that "Men who have used violence even once have an additional power resource and are therefore more likely to be found in marriages the spouses' judged to be husband dominated" [47:22]. It is unfortunate that Adler's sample is so small, but it nevertheless gives us some hint of how wife-beating may be related to male domination of decision-making processes in what are considered normal U.S. families. This process is, in a sense, a special case of Patterson's coercion theory [94], in which negative behaviors are used by family members to coerce each other.

Solutions to Wife-Beating

The purpose of the research reported in the following chapters is not to establish any additional facts about the nature and extent of U.S. wife-beating. Instead, its purpose is to find out what beaten wives do to relieve themselves of the problem. Among the possible acts are: (1) calling the police, (2) seeking professional counseling, (3) entering a shelter for battered women, (4) leaving home for good and seeking a divorce, (5) fighting back, and (6) convincing one's husband one's self or with the help of informal support networks, to cease his assaultive behavior. These possibilities are not mutually exclusive. Several of them may be followed at the same time or used in succession.

There is a considerable literature on the use of police to help in domestic disputes. In a sense, calling the police is a poor tactical choice for beaten wives, in view of the fact that they are generally untrained in handling marital disputes and may be uninterested in following through on the case [95, 96, 97]. However, the increasing emphasis on family-crisis intervention by the police [98, 99, 100, 101, 102] has improved the situation somewhat in many of the larger cities. It is clear that the volume of domestic-violence cases handled by the police is considerable [2, 5, 6, 90] but there are substantial differences in the estimates of the proportion of wives who utilize the police after or during a beating incident. Thirty-two percent of the women studied by Gayford [22], thirty-six percent of the women surveyed by Carlson [24], and more than half of the women in the sample examined by Flynn [103] had utilized the police at some time for physical protection from their husbands. Fields [18], Oppenlander [104], and Walker [65] point out the difficulties that women have in seeking relief from wife-beating through contacts with police officers. The police play a calming and listening role, and are available to assist victims by taking them to the hospital or by protecting them while they pack up and leave the house [8]. However, difficulties arise when women try to press charges and obtain convictions. Further problems result from the limited protection that police can provide to the victim of wife-beating. Unless she seeks help beyond that which can be provided by police officers, she will be vulnerable to further marital assaults as soon as the police leave the house.

The second avenue of relief—psychological and medical help—has received modest attention from researchers in recent years. Flynn [103] found that two-thirds of the wife-beating victims had received counseling from marriage counselors or the clergy at one point in their marriages, and Gayford [22] found that 57 percent of his subjects had previously sought help from social services. In contrast, very few of the women studied by Carlson [24] and Ashley [43] had utilized social services or mental-health agencies. There is some indication that once battered women do make contact with a counseling source, they persist for a larger number of sessions than other clients [20], which indicates the seriousness with which they regard the problem. Dobash and Dobash [6] found that women who attended physicians for their injuries after wife-beating incidents were rarely referred to appropriate sources for additional help. They offer a scathing criticism of both medical and counseling practitioners for the limited value of their services to many victims of wife-beating.

A more general problem is that counselors are rarely able to work directly with the abusing husband. Wisconsin statistics gathered by Anderson, Sweet, and Lythcott [11] show that while community agencies provided counseling to 84 percent of the spouse-abuse victims who sought their help, they counselled the aggressor in these situations only 8 out of 1,618 cases. Although counseling may aid the beaten wife in deciding what to do with her life and perhaps offer suggestions as to how to deal with her husband's violence, the structure of the situation makes it difficult for counseling to deal with the problem more directly.

The third possible form of relief, the use of shelters (or refuges, as they are called in Great Britain) offers no permanent solution to the problem of wife-beating. Shelters are places where women go for protection, to recover, to obtain counseling and other support services, and to determine future plans. The development of the shelter as a resource for battered women is quite recent. The first shelter in Great Britain did not open until the early 1970s [41, 42, 105], and the development of shelters in the United States is even more recent [65, 106]. Once shelters began to be established in the United States, they were heavily used. For example, in Wisconsin 489 women received shelter care provided by community agencies and social-service departments in 1976 [11]. More than one thousand women stayed at the Rainbow Retreat in Phoenix over a three year period, and the Haven Shelter in Pasadena has been operating at full capacity since 1972 [107]. Despite the rapid development of the U.S. shelter movement, the latest directory of shelter services assembled by the Center for Women Policy Studies [108] shows that some states have only two or three shelters. It is fair to say that no state has enough shelters to meet the needs of its battered women. Papers by Ferraro [28, 29, 109], and articles by Marcovitch [110], Vaughan [37], Ashley [43] and Lowenberg [111] describe how these shelters attempt to protect the beaten wives from their aggressive husbands and at the same time to offer them multidisciplinary rehabilitative services.

How commonly do the victims of wife-beating choose to leave their mates and seek either a long-term separation or divorce? Statistics collected by Gaquin [84], O'Brien [15] and Levinger [16] imply that divorce is fairly common in families that experience wife-beating. Flynn's [103] more informal study of the opinions of court workers and attorneys yielded estimates that from 10 to 50 percent of all divorce cases involved some degree of wife-beating. Many women leave home only to return again for such reasons as coercion or promises of reform from their husbands, concern for their children, or lack of resources to support themselves independently. Gayford [22] reports that 81 percent of the women he studied had left their husbands on more than one occasion. Thirty-six percent had left their husbands more than four times. Relatives were the most common source of shelter, with a small number of women going to friends or seeking other accommodations. When Gelles [57] compared abused women who left home with abused women who stayed, he found that the leavers tended to have been more severely abused, were less likely to have experienced violence as a child, and had higher educational and occupational status. Using data collected by Walker [66], Nielsen et al. [68] found that the less socially isolated the battered wife, the longer she stayed in the marital relationship. Even when a woman successfully leaves a wife-beater, she may not be free from his attacks. Carlson [24] comments that many divorced women are actively sought out by their ex-husbands for continued abuse.

A fifth response to wife-beating is to overtly return the violence. This is not a common response, as men are usually bigger and stronger then their wives [47] and also better trained in methods of self-defense and physical aggression [112]. Women who respond to violence with violence are placed by Pfouts [19] into her category of the aggressive wife. Only 8 percent of the women studied by Gayford [22] fought back when their husbands attacked them. Carlson [24] reports that 77 percent of the women attempted to defend themselves against their husbands' attacks, but it is not clear to what extent this self-defense involved overt aggression against their husbands. The research evidence also is unclear as to the effectiveness of this technique. Most of Carlson's respondents felt that self-defense led to an increased intensity of the husband's violence. This too is what one would expect from Dibble and Straus's [76] finding that being hit by one's spouse provides moral sanction or justification for one's own violence towards the spouse. In contrast, Pagelow [113] found that the small proportion of the women in her sample who decided to fight violence with violence were successful in every case except one. One of these women rendered her husband unconscious by striking him with an iron skillet, and a second kicked her husband in the groin. In the most remarkable case, a beaten wife waited until her drunken husband fell asleep, and awakened him with a knife at his throat, telling him that if he ever beat her again she would wait until he fell asleep and kill him.

Many beaten wives never consult the helping professions, do not call the police or take refuge in shelters, and do not get a divorce. They are afraid to fight back, and yet their husbands continue to beat them. These women must find some other way of inhibiting their husbands' physical aggression toward them, perhaps with the help of their neighbors, family members, or other contacts in informal helping networks. As Pagelow points out, "Until very recently, untold millions of women were limited to the alternative of staying and attempting change from within, largely because when they tried to get external help, they received negative institutional response and lacked necessary resources for leaving" [113:7].

Carlson [24] reports that except for their use of the police, the battered women he studied relied primarily on informal networks for obtaining sympathy or assistance. In her sample, six times as many women consulted a friend or family member as a social-service or mental-health agency, and the number consulting a religious adviser was even smaller. Women's groups were consulted almost as often as family and friends, and these three sources together made up a larger proportion of the resources used by the beaten wives then any other help-source. Two-thirds of the women studied by Flynn [103] reported relying on family and friends for emotional support and sometimes for emergency shelter after experiencing conjugal assault. Scott [114] believes that the absence of the informal resources provided by the extended family deprives a wife and her children of their natural allies in a marital conflict, leaving them vulnerable to their husbands. A recent analysis of national survey data by Cazenave and Straus [74] shows that violence is higher in families that have recently moved than in those living in the same neighborhood for three or more years. This supports the notion of an inverse relationship between informal support networks and family violence.

In his theoretical article on force and violence in family units, Goode [1] says that friends, neighbors, and family members traditionally intervene in family disputes to keep the peace, using threats and even force if necessary. He gives the example of neighbors pounding on the apartment wall of a couple having a violent argument. The pounding constitutes a threat that the police will be called if the level of conflict is not modulated. In contrast, an experimental study by O'Neil [115] found that only 47 percent of his subjects would report an incident of family violence occurring next door. Blacks (55 percent) were more likely to report a nearby incident of family violence than whites (42 percent), and neighbors with grammar school or less education (65 percent) had a greater probability of reporting incidents than those with some college background (40 percent). Neighborhoods in which many people knew each other were more likely to produce calls to the police

(49 percent) than those in which people did not know their neighbors (39 percent).

The support and advice offered by friends and family members to the beaten wife may influence her to utilize social services in the community or to take actions herself to relieve the problem. In an unpublished doctoral dissertation O'Farrell [116] found that family and friends were influential in women's decisions to separate·from their husbands. Wives may also be influenced by such support groups to fight back. Dibble and Straus [76] found that respondents who had held a nonviolent attitude before they were hit by their spouses but who consulted relatives and friends after they were beaten were more likely to engage in violence themselves, presumably of a defensive nature, than those who did not talk to relatives and friends (59 percent versus 49 percent). Unfortunately, this finding is not broken down by sex of victim, so it is not clear to what extent this pattern holds for wives as compared with husbands. In any case, it is certainly true that a husband's informal contacts might influence him to become more violent toward his wife, just as a wife's informal contacts might influence her to defend herself more effectively against her husband. Dibble and Straus summarize their research on informal networks with the statement that " . . . involvement in a personal network of friends and relatives can support not only acts which are normative but also acts which are clearly deviant as far as the 'standard' norms of the society are concerned" [11].

Social Networks and their Resources

There is a small, but steadily growing amount of literature on self-help groups and informal social networks. This literature has tended to see self-help activities as leading to or supplementing therapeutic intervention by professionals, rather than as a valid and effective alternative to it [117]. A second problem with this literature is that most general publications on self-help groups and informal social networks completely ignore wife-beating as a problem that might be dealt with through such avenues. For example, the Task Panel Report on helping networks that was submitted to the President's Commission on Mental Health lists concerns such as bereavement, care of elderly, first pregnancy, major illness in patient or immediate family, adolescents, being a newcomer to the community, and being a multi-problem family as situations to be dealt with through social networks; but there is no mention of family violence in connection with helping networks [118].

Self-help groups have been prominent on the U.S. scene ever since Alcoholics Anonymous began in 1935 [119]. Through these groups, people with similar problems are able to come together to exchange accounts of their experiences, to obtain information about how to deal with their situations, and to receive much needed social support to overcome temporary setbacks and restructure lifestyles [120, 121, 122]. Levy [123] identifies eleven processes that occur in self-help groups, and Katz [124] mentions nine. Some of the crucial factors mentioned by these authors are that (1) self-help groups provide new members with successful models of coping with stress through their interactions with program leaders, (2) relations in a group occur at the horizontal or peer level rather than in a vertical status system, (3) groups provide an entire substitute culture and social structure that supports new definitions of the situation and new personal identities, and that (4) groups award status for problem-solving success rather than for the socioeconomic criteria used in the general society. Hurvitz [quoted in 104] brings these characteristics into sharp relief with his list of eighty-eight differences between conventional psychotherapy and self-help peer psychotherapy groups.

In a more parsimonious discussion of the differences between self-help groups and professional counseling, Durman [125] points to the factors of support, advocacy, and normalizing. He argues that self-help groups provide a great deal more support for their members than counselors do for their clients. These groups are also willing to stand up and advocate the rights of their members. While many professional counselors tend to see the needs presented by clients as indicating deeper problems, members of self-help groups tend to normalize these needs by seeing them as reflecting immediate circumstances rather than deeper problems. Because the circumstances are viewed as relatively short-term, action that is simple, direct, and specific to the need presented is all that is required.

Self-help groups represent an intermediate step between professional services and help obtained through informal social networks. Whereas self-help groups have a formal social structure and exist to serve specific purposes, natural support-systems have a more informal structure and offer support over a broad range of needs. Henderson [126] points out that informal networks, particularly those consisting of family members, rise to a peak of prominence whenever there is a community disaster as well as an individually expressed need. There is some evidence that psychological symptom levels in the face of serious life events are minimized by immersion in a network of social support [127]. Cobb [128] believes that the observed protective effects of social support-networks operate through the facilitation of coping and adaptation to the environment. Coping, which involves manipulating the environment to meet the needs of the self, and adaptation, which is changing the self to produce a more effective actor in the environment, complement each other in the self's movement toward problem definition and solution. Gottlieb [129] outlines eleven problem-solving behaviors that occur in informal social-support networks, plus the possibility of direct environmental action to reduce the source of stress. The problem-solving behaviors are (1) focused talking, (2) clarifying problems, (3) suggesting the means of problem-solving, (4) issuing directives for problem-solving, (5) providing information about the source of stress, (6) referring members to other helping resources, (7) ensuring compliance with problem-solving directives, (8) offering protection from sources of stress, (9) modeling successful behavior or providing testimony about successful behavior, (10) providing material aid for direct service, and (11) distracting members from excessively focusing on problems. Recent research suggests that self-help and informal-network processes in such disparate areas as physical health [130, 131] and consumer dispute resolution [132, 133] have the same characteristics as self-help and informal-network processes in mental health.

Two problems exist when considering using informal social networks: First, the networks may themselves be sources of additional problems for an individual [134, 135]; and second, many of the people who have a strong need for support may have a negative orientation toward social networks. As Tolsdorf [134] points out, many individuals go through life without drawing on the advice, support, or feedback of individuals in their social networks. This may be because of (1) embarrassment at admitting to having problems, (2) feeling a sense of damaged pride, (3) believing that members of the network do not have the appropriate expertise to help, or (4) anticipating that the network will give responses which the person wishes to avoid. In Tolsdorf's research, medical subjects were less likely than psychiatric patients to reject the use of social network support-services. This could mean that the utilization of support-network services is related to specific personality types or, alternatively, that it is related to the types of problems experienced by subjects. Another possibility is that network utilization may be related to one's status within the network.

Finlayson's [136] research on the use of social networks in Scotland by wives of heart-attack patients gives us some idea of the relative use of different help-sources. When the wives were interviewed at the time of the crisis, 16 percent of them expected that they would utilize the resources of non-professional others. These others comprised neighbors, fellow workers, and friends. The women were equally likely to expect to consult their children, less likely to expect to consult professionals and their husband's relatives, and much more likely to expect to consult their husband or their own relatives. In a follow-up after twelve months, the percentage of wives consulting others stayed exactly the same, the use of children, husband and husband's family increased, and the use of wife's family decreased as compared with their expectations in the first interview. There was a tendency for middle-class wives of successfully recovered husbands to have utilized support from non-professional others more often than working-class wives. In addition, U.S. study of the help-sources sought by adolescent mothers for a wide variety of problems showed a heavy use of family sources (70 percent of all cases) and agency sources (53 percent), but a surprisingly low use of friends (15 percent) for help [137].

Two studies that come even closer to the situation of wife-beating were conducted by Leiberman and Bond [138] and McKinlay [139]. McKinlay collected data on the use of social networks by families in Aberdeen, Scotland. Five specific problem-areas were discussed with the families, and detailed data are presented on four of these five areas in the article. The only area that is ignored in the article is "quarreling with ones husband," which was not discussed with women who were interviewed in the presence of their husbands. Because of the smaller numbers, McKinlay gives us no information about social-network resource utilization in this kind of situation. Wife-beating, a much more severe crisis, was not included in the survey.

In the other article, Leiberman and Bond present data on participation in consciousness-raising groups by 1,668 women who were haphazardly rather than randomly selected. The most important reason for joining a consciousness-raising group was interest in women's issues, but the second and third most important reasons were to seek help and to meet social needs. Help-seeking questionnaire items included (1) finding relief from things or feelings troubling the respondent, (2) solving personal problems, (3) dealing with current life-problems, and (4) bringing about some change in self. Social needs included making friends, loneliness, and finding a community in which one could participate. Although wife-beating was not specifically included in the questionnaire, it appears that the help-seeking items tapped many women whose experience as beaten wives accounted for their participation. When identifying the kind of woman who would benefit from involvement in consciousness-raising groups, respondents commonly cited the woman in an unstable marriage. This again subsumes beaten wives without mentioning them specifically. The efficacy of feminist treatment is given further support by McShane and Oliver [140], who detailed the differences in services that can be provided by feminist and non-feminist groups.

This brief excursion into the literature of self-help groups and informal social networks shows that valuable typological work has been done in both areas. However, no large-scale studies of sufficient scope have been conducted to offer a fundamental understanding of the operation of either of these helping resources, and only a few hints [1, 24, 76, 115, 116] are available as to the way in which self-help groups and informal social networks are utilized by beaten wives to cope with abusive situations. Furthermore, publications on sources of help for battered wives rarely mention the use of informal networks, although it is more likely that references will be made to feminist self-help groups. Crowley et al. [141] offer a discouraging summary of the value of families, friends, and neighbors to battered women. The work of Wahler [142] suggests that the isolation of wives from positive social-network contact is greater in the lower class than in the middle class and that it is associated with family problems other than marital violence. The most positive comment on the matter is by Straus [77], who says that it is important to obtain advice, assistance, and moral support from one's neighbors, relatives, and friends because these people can offer assistance in the form of specific suggestions, aid in settling disputes, and often physical sanctuary. Straus points out that the beaten wife who avoids involving these people gives the husband a psychological advantage by insulating him from shame and the criticism of his behavior by community members.

2

The Milwaukee Study

The prevalence of wife-beating in the United States as a whole and in numerous states and communities has already been estimated. Random-sample survey techniques have been used to produce incidence rates and background information on the problem, although they have not been able to provide a sophisticated understanding of the causes and dynamics underlying wife-beating incidents.

Existing research has also demonstrated that wife-beating is a serious social problem in the United States. The severity of the physical injuries inflicted on many spouses, the relationship between wife-beating and child abuse, the relative ineffectiveness of the criminal-justice system in responding to the needs of beaten wives, and the contribution of marital violence to separation and divorce have been adequately documented. The long-term psychological and social effects of wife-beating are less fully understood, and we are just beginning to explore its implications for marital power and family dispute resolution.

Although previous research has established the prevalence and seriousness of wife-beating in the United States, it has not yet successfully determined how the victim can remain in her own home and minimize her risk of continued abuse. Many researchers do not recruit subjects for study until after these beaten wives have already left their marriages. Even when subjects are recruited from intact marriages, they are usually perceived by researchers as unable to deal with their victimization without professional help. The few existing random-sample surveys focusing on marital violence have not located large numbers of subjects who have solved the problem in their own lives, nor have these surveys focused on the techniques and strategies used by those wives who have been successful in defeating wife-beating. As a result of such gaps in the existing literature, it is difficult to offer advice to women who are currently experiencing marital violence, but who would like to deal with the violence in ways other than leaving the home. Numerous conversations with counselors, lawyers, and other professionals working with beaten wives on a daily basis confirm that they generally feel helpless to give advice about beating wife-beating. They usually indicate that the only thing a repeatedly battered wife can do is leave her marriage.

Our research is designed to fill the gap in the existing literature created by the lack of information on the strategies and help-sources used by beaten wives to triumph over violence in their marriages. This is not only a scholarly exercise it also meets an important human need. The work of Straus et al. [82] suggests that there are millions of beaten spouses in the United States today who could benefit from a much wider range of options than those expressed by the phrases "grin and bear it" and "see your lawyer." To address this need, our research is designed to discover realistic options for the nuclear family.

A rough comparison between the Straus incidence data and treatment utilization statistics suggests that most women who experience wife-beating do not choose to consult the police or social-service agencies. The national incidence of wife-beating is so high that if all victims asked for help from formal treatment sources, these sources would be overwhelmed. Beyond this, many women find using these resources personally unacceptable for a variety of reasons. Considering these factors, it is appropriate that our research primarily focuses on self-help and informal social-network support in combating wife-beating.

There is a great ground swell of concern about marital violence in this country. It has its roots not only in feminism, but also in tenets of some major U.S. religions, and in the increasing recognition of the political importance of women in national affairs. Shelters for battered women, feminist counseling-services, self-help groups, social support-networks, and many other kinds of organizations are proliferating at a rapid rate, although they are still meeting only a small portion of the existing need for these services. The general problem is that services are developing more rapidly than knowledge of the subject, so that both the professional and common-sense knowledge available to these organizations is not adequate to the task at hand. Our project relates to this problem in that one of its long-term objectives is to provide knowledge of strategies and techniques useful in defeating wife-beating to professionals and to informal social support-networks.

A second long-range objective is to increase the self-confidence of battered women. Women cannot hope to overcome violence in their marriages unless they feel confident that they have the ability to do so. Existing research tends to reinforce the image of beaten wives as being relatively incompetent and unsuccessful in dealing with marital violence. Like most of the existing research on other kinds of victimization, these studies do not pay sufficient attention to the creative and persistent efforts of the victims to gain control over their own lives and to deal effectively with their victimizers. Our research is designed to determine whether or not women can be located who were beaten by their mates, and who having struggled creatively and extensively with the violence, eventually triumphed over it. It is our intent to encourage beaten wives and battering husbands to actively seek solutions to the problem of marital violence to the best of their abilities.

A final long-term objective of our research is to provide a basis for policy development at the local, state, and national levels. It is not just a matter of what is the best advice to give to beaten wives. There is the problem of how best to deliver supportive services. What is the most efficient packaging for supportive services? What should the split of resources be between professional support-services and self-help and social network support-services? Which of the conditions of marital violence are most amenable to self-help and social network help-sources, and which require a greater emphasis on the use of professional help-sources? Our research is designed to address these and numerous other policy questions.

Recruiting the Sample

Our initial choice of a city for the exploratory study was Racine, Wisconsin. Although Racine has less than one hundred thousand inhabitants, we hoped that we could draw enough interview subjects to complete the study. We intended to use Milwaukee for a later, more extensive study, and we therefore preferred to avoid that city in the exploratory study. During the first months of the grant, we contacted fifty-six Racine social-service agencies and other community organizations, five newspapers, four radio stations, and one television station. The organizations included churches, social work and counseling agencies, educational institutions, organizations fighting racism and sexism, coordination and planning organizations, self-help groups, crisis lines, and agencies fostering community organizations. The sum total of all recruitment activities in Racine produced only ten interviews in three months, so we made the decision to switch our study site to Milwaukee. Although we did not fully exhaust our resources in Racine, it is clear that the project would never have succeeded in recruiting enough subjects if activities had been limited to the Racine area.

The small population of Racine limited subject recruitment to some degree. More importantly, however, its small-town psychology made potential subjects much more leary of participating in the project than they would have been had they lived in a large urban area. Racine appears to be more ideologically conservative than Milwaukee and is dominated by a neighborhood orientation that renders potential subjects unwilling to raise suspicions about their family among their neighbors. Informal comments by Racine residents indicate that the pervasive sense of knowing one another's business makes it difficult for potential subjects to have faith in the promised guarantee of confidentiality and anonymity.

It was our judgment that the lack of response from Racine was not due to deficiencies in our strategy for subject recruitment but was rather due to the characteristics of the local community. We concluded that our methodology would not be successful in small communities and probably would not be successful in rural areas either. Rather than change our methodology and continue to base our research in Racine, we determined to continue to test our methodology and to move our research site to a larger community.

Relocation to Milwaukee

We succeeded in making contacts with 122 Milwaukee social agencies and other organizational units in the first two months of our Milwaukee campaign. Contacts were also made with twenty-eight newspapers and newsletters, thirteen radio stations, and six television stations. A total of thirty-one personal appearances were made before groups and classes, and appearances were made on five radio talk shows and two television talk shows. The community organization experiences and agency contacts of the School of Social Welfare at the University of Wisconsin—Milwaukee permitted us to move quickly into the Milwaukee community and to receive considerable community support for our efforts. In addition to the two major daily Milwaukee newspapers, we received coverage in student newspapers, neighborhood newspapers, and newspapers appealing to special religious and cultural groups.

Within three months, free announcements had appeared in at least ten Milwaukee newspapers and newsletters. Many of these publications gave generous coverage to the project, and editorial comment on the project was enthusiastic. A number of Milwaukee radio stations carried public-service announcements about the project, and one radio station broadcast an editorial supporting the project eighteen times. After the intensity of this initial campaign, we settled into a pattern of placing newspaper advertisements every few weeks and keeping in contact with media personnel. We received excellent coverage by the two most popular social-issues commentators on Milwaukee network television stations, and had letters published three times in the area's most popular newspaper advice column. An example of the style of our newspaper advertisements is presented in figure 2–1. The advertisements appeared in the two major Milwaukee newspapers (*Milwaukee Journal*, *Milwaukee Sentinel*) plus numerous student and community newspapers, some with a specific minority focus. In total, there were nine months of active recruitment in Milwaukee, which produced 136 interviews.

As a check on our recruiting strategies, we asked our subjects to tell us how they heard about the project, how quickly they contacted us after hearing about it, whether the former batterer knew about their participation, and if he did, what his reaction to it was. The first contact that the

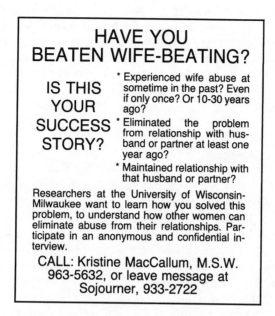

Figure 2–1. Newspaper Advertisement for Subject Recruitment

subjects had with the study was generally through newspaper advice columns and editorials (51 percent) or through newspaper advertisements (34 percent); with television and radio far behind (7 percent); and personal presentations, posters, and word-of-mouth accounting for the remaining subjects. Fifty-five percent of the subjects contacted us after they first heard about the project; 21 percent had to hear about it several times before contacting us; 14 percent discussed the project with their friends after hearing about it, and then decided to contact us; and 10 percent did not contact us until after discussing it with their husbands. The former batterer knew about the victim's participation in the study in 27 percent of the cases, approving readily in half of these and reluctantly in the other half.

Do specific recruitment techniques appeal more to one category of subjects than to another? Bivariate analyses of the relationships between fifteen demographic and violence characteristics (income, occupation, religion, religiosity, age, recreational organization involvement, violence from parents, premarital violence, marital violence, et cetera) and how the subject first heard of the project yielded correlations very close to zero, ranging from -.06 to .11. A similar pattern emerged when these variables were cross-tabulated with how quickly the subjects contacted the project. However, there was a slight tendency (Tau b = .14) for women with no college experience to be more likely than women with some college experience or those with a college degree to contact the project after first hearing about it. College graduates were more likely than the other subjects to want to discuss participating in the project with friends or their husbands before contacting project staff. With this single exception, it appears that our various techniques for attracting volunteers had similar success with women of a broad range of ages, income levels, religious involvements, and so forth.

Interviewing Procedures

To be included in the sample, a woman had to have been physically beaten at least once by a person with whom she was married or cohabiting at the time of the violence. In addition, she had to have triumphed over the violence, with or without the help of the aggressor. To assure that some degree of success had in fact occurred, subjects were not accepted into the sample unless the violence had ended at least one year prior to the interview.

In-depth interviews were conducted informally, following an interview guide rather than a formal questionnaire. Questions were asked differently according to the characteristics of the subjects and the interviewing situation, and the interviewer probed at will to obtain appropriate details about each incident or variable included in the interview guide. When a given topic was too delicate to press at one point in the interview, it was skipped and the interviewer returned to it at a later time when rapport had been strengthened. When there was some doubt about the authenticity of some information, or a problem with recall, the interviewer asked about the same information at different points in the interview and reconciled the inconsistencies with the interviewee. The combination of probing, repeating questions, and reconciling inconsistencies minimized the problem of recall that exists in retrospective studies such as this one. When it was apparent that the information recalled was vague and that inconsistencies would not be satisfactorily reconciled, the entire interview was removed from the data set. We were lucky that this was necessary in only two cases.

In order to provide round-the-clock phone service, the project contracted with a local battered-women's shelter having a crisis hotline to receive calls during off-hours. Once phone contact was made between the interviewer and a subject, the interview appointment was set, and the subject was given a choice of an interview in university offices, at a neutral site such as a church or library, or in the subject's own home. There were only twelve occasions on which subjects failed to appear for interviews without previously rescheduling the time with the interviewer.

The categories for the analysis of the data were developed from the responses of the subjects. This meant that the coding scheme for the variables was constantly in flux, with new values being added to some of the variables and entirely new variables being created occasionally. Two exceptions were violence suffered and help received. Although the subjects described these topics in their own words, their responses were coded using standard scales to permit comparisons among different violent incidents (including intergenerational comparisons) and various formal and informal help-sources. The values for the content of help received were taken from the classification scheme of informal helping behaviors developed by Gottlieb [129]. These values are displayed in figure 2–2. The violent incidents were measured using an elaboration of the conflict tactics scale used by Straus, Gelles and Steinmetz [82] (see figure 2–3). This elaboration retained the structure of the conflict tactics scale to permit comparisons between the Milwaukee data and the national survey data on family violence that is being analyzed by Straus and his associates at the University of New Hampshire.

Subjects had the study and their rights as participants fully explained to them before agreeing to participate in the interview. In order to guard their anonymity, they signed a consent form with four random digits of their choosing rather than with their own names. No record of the names of the interviewees was kept in the project's files. Although the subjects understood that they could break off the interview at any point, none of them selected to do so. Subjects were given referral information in case they became upset by the interview, but to the best of our knowledge, there were no negative reactions strong enough to stimulate the use of the referral information. It was never necessary to ask Dr. Elam Nunnally, who had agreed to offer counseling support to subjects, to provide emergency counseling for any of the interviewees. We presume that those who did not feel that they could cope with the stress of the interview elected not to respond to our media presentations.

Sample Characteristics

In all but six of the couples studied, the information was exclusively provided by the wife. All of the couples were heterosexual, and 94 percent were legally married during the period covered by the interviews. In this report, the subjects and their ex-batterers are referred to as husband and wife, even though a few of the couples were never legally married. Ninety-two percent of the women had one or more siblings in their family of orientation, and 82 percent were raised entirely by their natural parents. Twenty-eight percent of their fathers were professionals or managers, 35 percent were craftsmen, salesmen, or foremen, and the remainder worked as farmers, services workers, or laborers. Half of their mothers were homemakers, 10 percent

Code Values	Value Descriptions
(01)	Unfocused talking
(02)	Providing reassurance
(03)	Providing encouragement
(04)	Listening
(05)	Showing understanding
(06)	Showing respect
(07)	Showing concern
(08)	Showing trust
(09)	Reflecting intimacy
(10)	Providing companionship
(11)	Providing accompaniment in a stressful situation
(12)	Providing an extended period of care
(13)	Focused talking
(14)	Providing clarification of problems
(15)	Providing suggestions about the means of problem-solving
(16)	Commanding or directing the wife about problem-solving
(17)	Providing information about the source of stress
(18)	Providing referral to alternative helping sources: lawyer, shelter, et cetera
(19)	Assuring that the wife complies with problem-solving directives
(20)	Buffering the wife from source of stress
(21)	Models or provides testimony of own experience
(22)	Provides material aid and/or other direct service
(23)	Distracts wife's attention from focusing excessively on the problem
(24)	Indicates unconditional availability to the wife
(25)	Indicates readiness to act in the wife's best interest
(26)	Intervenes directly in the environment to diminish the source of stress
(27)	Other, please describe
(99)	Not applicable
(00)	Missing data

Figure 2–2. Helping-Behaviors Scale

Code Values	Value Descriptions
(01)	Tried to discuss the issue calmly
(02)	Did discuss the issue calmly
(03)	He got information to support his side
(04)	I got information to support my side
(05)	He brought in someone else to try and help settle things
(06)	I brought in someone else to try and help settle things
(07)	He argued a lot but did not yell or scream
(08)	I argued a lot but did not yell or scream
(09)	He cried
(10)	I cried
(11)	He yelled, screamed, or insulted me
(12)	I yelled, screamed, or insulted him
(13)	He sulked and refused to talk about it
(14)	I sulked and refused to talk about it
(15)	He stomped out of the room
(16)	I stomped out of the room
(17)	He threw something (but not at me) or smashed something
(18)	I threw something (but not at him) or smashed something
(19)	He threatened to hit or throw something at me
(20)	I threatened to hit or throw something at him
(21)	He threw something at me
(22)	I threw something at him
(23)	He pushed, grabbed, or shoved me
(24)	I pushed, grabbed, or shoved him
(25)	He hit me with a hand
(26)	I hit him with a hand
(27)	He hit (or tried to hit) me with something hard, not a hand
(28)	I hit (or tried to hit) him with something hard, not a hand
(29)	He kicked, bit, or hit me with a fist
(30)	I kicked, bit, or hit him with a fist
(31)	He threatened to break up the marriage by separation or divorce
(32)	I threatened to break up the marriage by separation

Figure 2–3. Violence Scale

Figure 2–3. *continued*

Code Values	Value Descriptions
	or divorce
(33)	He beat me up
(34)	I beat him up
(35)	He threatened to use a knife or gun
(36)	I threatened to use a knife or gun
(37)	He assaulted me with a knife
(38)	I assaulted him with a knife
(39)	He assaulted me with a gun
(40)	I assaulted him with a gun
(41)	Other: please describe
(99)	Not applicable
(00)	Missing data

were professionals or managers, 16 percent worked as secretaries or in sales, and 14 percent worked as operatives or service workers. In their own marriages, as many women were service workers as homemakers (22 percent in each case), 20 percent were clericals, and 14 percent were professionals or managers.

The mean age of the once-battered women was thirty-eight, with 27 percent being age thirty or younger and 16 percent being over fifty-years old. There were only twelve minority subjects, seven of them black. Forty-five percent of the women reported were Protestant, 41 percent Catholic, and 12 percent said that they had no religion at all. Just over half the women attended church weekly, and a similar proportion had completed at least one college course. One out of every five women had received a four-year college degree.

During their marriages, the subjects had been involved in an average of three organized recreational activities, the most common of which were educational classes (36 percent of all subjects), church-sponsored activities (30 percent), and sports (23 percent). They had an average of 2.1 children with former batterers, and 16 percent brought additional children with them from a previous relationship. The average couple had moved five times during their relationship, and the mean time at the current address was 4.8 years.

The husbands or partners in the battering relationships had at least one sibling in their family of orientation in 93 percent of the cases, and 74 percent were raised entirely by their natural parents. Their fathers had slightly lower-status occupations than the fathers of their wives: 20 percent professionals or managers, 36 percent craftsmen, salesmen, or foremen, and 44 percent service workers, farmers, or laborers. Their mothers were more likely than their wives' mothers to be homemakers (63 percent) and slightly less likely to be professionals or managers (7 percent). In their own marriages, they were most likely to be craftsmen or foremen (28 percent), managers or professionals (24 percent), and operatives (20 percent).

The husbands averaged three years older than their wives (age 41) and were more likely to report having no religion at all (25 percent). They were much less likely to attend church weekly than their wives (32 percent), and slightly less educated (46 percent with one or more college courses, 16 percent with a four-year college degree). Their level of organized recreational involvement was somewhat lower than their wives' (a mean of 2.4), with sports (25 percent) and educational classes (18 percent) the most common activities. One out of every eight husbands brought at least a single child from a previous relationship into the battering relationship. Just over half of the husbands had served in the armed forces, with an average length of service of three years, and 16 percent had seen combat.

Not all subjects were still living with the former batterers at the time of the interview. Half of those who had ever been married were no longer living with their husbands by then. Although most had successfully solved the violence problem while married, they found other reasons why the relationships with the ex-batterers were not worth continuing, and so they eventually divorced, in some cases many years after the cessation of the battering.

When interviewed in 1980 and 1981, the average family income of the subjects was $22,360. Twenty-nine percent of the family incomes were $25,000 or over (42 percent of the incomes of those who were still living with the ex-batterer, as compared with 15 percent of the incomes of those who left him). This illustrates the point that one of the costs of leaving an unsatisfactory relationship is often a lowered standard of living.

It is difficult to get a feel for the sample through the recitation of dry statistics. As a counter to the statistics just given, three composite case histories that are representative of the women in the Milwaukee sample are presented. Like the vignettes presented throughout this report, these histories carefully combine elements from different cases so as to protect the anonymity of the subjects, many of whom could be identified by the unique characteristics of their experiences with wife-beating and its cessation.

Sandra

For Sandra, violence was not a part of her childhood experience. She was raised in a large family where her father, a farmer, often drank to excess but became gentle and fun-loving when inebriated. Sandra graduated from college and since that time has worked at a personnel agency where she is the temporary personnel manager. Sandra's husband Bill was raised by his mother and aunt after his father died when he was seven. The youngest of four brothers, Bill was overprotected by his mother and lived at home until his third year of college, when he married for the first time. This marriage ended after one year, and Sandra later learned that Bill had been violent with his first wife. Following college, Bill became an accountant, and has had jobs with numerous employers since that time. The couple first met at a tavern through Sandra's sister. After a six-month courtship, they decided to marry. While dating, Sandra perceived no drinking problems in Bill, and they argued only rarely. The arguments were generally around Sandra's professional ambitions, which her mate found to be threatening. Good communication and strong feelings of love characterized their relationship, and they were married when Sandra was twenty-seven years old and her husband was thirty-one.

The first incident of violence occurred on their wedding night, when Sandra was struck by Bill while enroute to a motel. He had been drinking earlier in the day, but appeared to be sober by then. While in the car, he accused her of flirting with the best man and, when she objected, hit her from the driver's seat. Sandra's reaction was one of shock and fear at having made a potential mistake in her choice of a husband. The next morning, he apologized for his actions, and promised never to strike her again. They discussed the incident at length, Sandra stressing her intolerance of violence, and she felt confident it would not recur.

The newlyweds moved into the first floor of a duplex owned and shared by Bill's mother. He then began spending most of his free time with his mother, and she, in turn, scolded Sandra for not providing a more satisfactory home for her son. Sandra's mother-in-law further antagonized her by suggesting that her son's poor work history was due to Sandra's professional ambitions, and that Sandra should devote all of her available time to her family.

Two years later Sandra was battered for the second time, when she discussed her desire to return to school while maintaining her job. The episode ended when she began to cry and Bill left the room. With her baby daughter, Sandra left the home and spent the night with a friend. She discussed the incident and her concerns with her friend, who offered strong support and encouraged Sandra to come to her for help at any time. When Sandra returned home, she and Bill discussed his behavior, and she confronted him with the bruises she had suffered. Again, he apologized and promised never to strike her in the future. However, Bill resorted to violence several more times over the next year. After each of these episodes, he left to spend the night at his mother's home. She supported her son's actions, accusing Sandra of irresponsibility toward her family.

The final episode occurred during the third year of marriage, when Bill returned home late after drinking with friends. Sandra prepared a meal for him, which he complained about and threw on the floor. He then proceeded to hit her with plates, a chair, and his fists. The incident ended only when he saw his daughter observing the violence and crying. Sandra escaped with her daughter to the apartment of her friend, who sheltered them for a week. During that week Sandra contacted a local battered-women's center for advice, and learned of the options available in her situation. She also had lengthy discussions with her friend, who indicated she would support Sandra regardless of her decision. At this point, Sandra felt confident that she had control over her life and began to discuss her options with Bill. She firmly stated that she would no longer tolerate abuse, both for her own sake as well as her daughter's. She insisted that, if she were to return, they needed to reevaluate their responsibilities, and that Bill's mother could no longer influence their marital arrangement. Accepting responsibility and concern for his behavior, Bill agreed to work hard to improve their marriage. In the past three years, Sandra and Bill have resolved many of their problems around work and family through open communication. For the past year he has sought treatment from a counselor, who has helped him to improve his self-image, and has succeeded in getting him to appreciate Sandra's talents without feeling threatened.

Alice

Alice grew up in an upper-middle-class family. Her father worked as a business executive and her mother was a homemaker. The family was fairly close, and the parents and children talked out problems and concerns with each other in order to come to mutual agreements about solutions. During her childhood and adolescent years, Alice experienced and witnessed no violence in her family. At eighteen she left home to attend a year of college and to seek employment as a secretary.

Alice's husband Fred was raised in a blue-collar family by his father, a factory foreman, and his mother, who worked as a store clerk. Playing a dominant role in the family, his father was physically violent to his mother frequently, during periods when he drank excessively. Occasionally, the children were victims of their father's abuse as well. The future batterer completed eleventh grade and became involved in sales work for a major company immediately prior to marrying.

Alice and Fred dated for one year prior to the marriage, during which time no violence occurred. Alice recognized a potential problem of drinking and jealousy in Fred while they dated, and they argued about these issues on several occasions. However, Alice thought that marriage would solve such problems. They decided to marry when Alice became pregnant. At the time of the marriage, in 1961, she was twenty years old and he was twenty-one.

Violence began three months after the wedding. During that time, Alice was pregnant and Fred's drinking became heavier in response to his increasing responsibilities. He argued with her about housework, her feeling ill due to her pregnancy, his feeling neglected, and so forth. His violence regularly erupted during weekend drinking binges, when he would arrive home late at night from taverns and would strike Alice during arguments. At this early period, Alice employed personal defenses to protect herself, including hitting Fred in self-defense on one occasion, an action that was not repeated, as he became more violent in response. Other techniques she attempted included trying to talk Fred out of his abusive behavior, which brought no success; hiding in the basement or outside; and protecting herself with her hands and feet to reduce injury. Following abusive incidents, Fred neither apologized for his actions nor discussed violence as a problem to be confronted.

After one year of marriage, Alice discussed the situation with her mother, who commented about her daughter's bruises. However, Alice's mother offered minimal help and was reluctant to become involved in her daughter's affairs. Thus, Alice determined she would have to search for help elsewhere. During the second marital year, Fred became progressively more violent, with incidents becoming more frequent and severe. There were several occasions on which he raped her after beating her up, and there might have been more sexual assaults had she resisted his advances more frequently. He also began striking their eldest son. At such times, Alice would go to her son's defense and invariably become a victim herself. Alice called the police for help several times during or following these incidents, but they provided little assistance. Most often, the officers would speak with Fred and Alice to calm the situation but would offer Alice no clear alternative to her predicament. During one police visit, an officer told her that unless the police actually witnessed the abuse they could do nothing legally to help her. Generally, after the police left the home, Fred calmed down, but he once retaliated with violence so severely that she feared calling upon the police again.

On one occasion, a neighbor witnessed an episode and intervened on Alice's behalf. From that point, she confided her concerns to her neighbor, who suggested that she become involved in Alanon for support. Alice started attending Alanon meetings in 1968, where she received tremendous support from other members in situations and with experiences like her own. During her involvement with Alanon, she learned that Fred's drinking and violence were not provoked by her actions, and that any change in his behavior had to be accomplished by him. Fred was threatened by her Alanon involvement and intensified his psychological abuse of her. Alice then was referred by an Alanon friend to a therapist for further help. This therapist successfully guided her toward discovering her strengths and talents and helped her to improve her self-image. From these experiences she gained the confidence to assert her independence more forcefully, despite Fred's attempts to block her efforts. She learned to drive a car, took a part-time job, and opened her own bank account.

The night of the final abusive incident, Fred had been drinking excessively. During an argument, he began battering Alice, and she sustained injuries. Both children attempted to intervene for her, the eldest son hitting his father with a toy truck in order to end the violence. Alice escaped to her neighbor's house with the children and called the police. The police arrived in ten minutes and offered support when she insisted that her husband be arrested. At the officer's suggestion, her neighbor rushed Alice to the hospital for documentation of injuries. From there Alice saw the district attorney and met an advocate from the local battered-women's center, who provided full information and support to her throughout the legal proceedings. Despite Fred's apologies and promises to cease further violence, Alice refused to drop the charges. Fred received one year's probation for assault and battery to his wife. Alice again approached her parents for help during this situation, and both responded with complete support. Her mother appeared at the trial and provided transportation and child care assistance when needed.

During the legal process, Alice filed for divorce and Fred left the home. Within a month after the trial, he recognized that the only recourse to reconciling his marriage was through alcohol treatment and counseling. He entered a one-month in-patient program for alcohol treatment, later participated in out-patient counseling, and also became involved in Alcoholics Anonymous (AA). While he was in treatment, the couple began discussing the problems in their marriage, and Alice agreed to drop the divorce if Fred would remain in counseling at AA. He continued his participation in therapy for two years, and has maintained his involvement in AA to the present day. There has been no violent episodes since the trial. Alice now describes their relationship as a very happy one, in which they enjoy common activities and interest and openly discuss and resolve problems.

Florence

Florence grew up in a low-income family. Her mother remarried while she was young, and both her natural father and her stepfather beat the mother and children. At a young age, she saw marriage as the only escape from her family. Her husband Jim's family was also violent. Jim's father, a factory worker, abused his mother and children, and the violence was both frequent and severe.

Florence and Jim met through friends, and dated for seven months before marrying. She agreed to marry Jim in order to escape her home situation, believing that he would care for her, and because, at the age of nineteen, she felt a great deal of love for him. While dating, Florence learned that Jim angered easily, often exhibiting a fierce temper. It was not uncommon for him to engage in fist fights with friends and family members. As a child and teenager, Jim had been a boxer at school and had spent time in a juvenile institution for his violent behavior. During the seven-month courtship, he slapped her a number of times, either after an argument in which he expressed extreme jealousy or when he had been drinking. On one occasion, he accused her of neglecting him at a party, after which he yelled at and slapped her. Another time, he hit Florence with his fists after she ran out of gas while enroute to pick him up from work. Florence broke up with Jim for a month after this episode, but they reconciled in response to his urgent pleading and apologies; she believed she could help him change. One month before the wedding, he beat her up again. Despite her inclination to cancel the wedding, she proceeded with the plans after her mother's promptings to overlook the incident as an isolated one which was not likely to be repeated. Florence entered the marriage fearing her husband, yet believing she could change his behavior.

The first incident of marital abuse occurred during their honeymoon. Very soon afterward, the abuse assumed a pattern of several incidents per week. Florence found it difficult to predict when these episodes would occur, for Jim would use force when drunk or sober, at any time during an argument, even when she was fast asleep in bed.

Two months into the marriage, following an abusive episode, Florence sought shelter at her parents' home. She returned to Jim after two weeks due to his incessant pleading, and because her parents discouraged a prolonged stay with them.

During the early period of abuse, Florence tried personal defense strategies, such as escaping or hiding, with little success. She eventually learned that avoiding Jim when his mood appeared potentially violent would occasionally bring her success. She was discouraged from discussing Jim's abuse with her parents because her mother, also a battered wife, was struggling with a similar problem, and she and her mother were never comfortable discussing personal problems. She did mention the problem several times to her sister, who listened to her concerns. However, her sister pointed to divorce as Florence's only alternative, which Florence rejected as a personal failure to meet her marital commitment. Several times she saw a clergyman for help but was told she must learn to better obey her husband and must work harder to keep him happy.

Over time, the frequency and severity of the battering increased, and the physical abuse was accompanied by intense and continuous psychological abuse. Florence's self-image sank to such depths that she feared performing such daily tasks as shopping alone. Further, she believed she was an incompetent mother and wife. With this self-perception, Florence began to believe she deserved Jim's abuse. One night, after a week of especially severe violence, and because she saw no other route of escape, she attempted suicide by overdosing on medication. She was taken to the hospital emergency room by her sister, and during her recovery began sessions with a psychiatrist. The psychiatrist, although somewhat supportive, did not focus on the abuse as the source of her depression. Eventually, the psychiatrist referred her to a mental-health self-help group, where she finally found support and understanding of her situation. Through this group, her self-esteem began to improve, and she began pursuing interests in church and other activities. She also discussd her marital situation with another church minister, who supported her efforts to pursue personal interests and identified the problem in the marriage as stemming from her husband. Jim's violence subsided somewhat because he recognized that his control over Florence was waning, and she now had friends who were openly supportive of her.

The last violent episode occured in 1979, in which Jim beat Florence with his fists during an argument. Her reaction was different from her earlier experiences in that something inside her clicked, signaling that she would no longer tolerate Jim's abuse. As he beat her, she actively defended herself, assaulted him with her fists, and injured him with a frying pan. After this incident, she threatened that any further attacks would bring about his arrest, that she would prefer charges and would divorce him without question. She also insisted on marriage counseling; both of them have participated in counseling for the past nine months.

Since the last violent incident, Jim has not exhibited any violence toward her. He has learned to better deal with his anger and frustrations by discussing problems with her, and by more openly communicating his feelings and worries. When his temper becomes peaked, he now temporarily leaves the room or the house. Although Florence sees many problems remaining in the relationship, she is confident that the violence will not recurr. And, in light of the progress which has been made by her husband, she is hopeful that he will learn to more fully accept and respect her as an equal in their marriage.

Data Analysis

Since the interviews lasted between two and four hours, the amount of information collected was voluminous. Where possible, this information was coded and computerized. The number of variables is huge because many of them recorded the same information for a series of incidents. For example, consider the helping services provided to the battered women by social-service agencies. Data were collected on the first, second, third, worst, and last incidents, plus a sixth incident designed to be a composite of all the remaining incidents. Since a subject might have contacted more than one social-service agency for help in relation to a particular incident, three possible contacts were allowed per incident, for a total of eighteen variables, all with the same help-content scale. In practice, the first contact in the worst incident and the first contact in the last incident were used in the bivariate analyses, but multiple response variables that summarized each series of parallel variables were also computed.

The variables used in this report are best conceived as falling into a series of blocks of variables. The largest block is the group of differentiating variables, which essentially set the background for the marital violence and its cessation. Differentiating variables include demographic characteristics, the social relations of the couple with friends and relatives, the experiences they had with violence in their families of orientation and other violence-sources outside of the battering relationship, the premarital violence that occurred in the battering relationship, and the characteristics of the battering relationship. A second block of variables describes the marital violence with respect to frequency, length, severity, and other relevant dimensions.

The marital violence descriptions are followed by four blocks of variables that describe and evaluate help-sources, techniques, and strategies used to combat the violence. These are the (1) wife's personal strategies and techniques, (2) informal help-sources, (3) formal help-sources, and (4) husband's efforts to end the violence. The wife's personal techniques and strategies include her own efforts to end the violence, such as talking, hiding, threatening, or aggressively fighting back. The informal help-sources examined in the study are friends, family members, in-laws, and neighbors. Formal help-sources include social-service agencies, the police, the clergy, and lawyers. The husband's efforts comprise all of these techniques, strategies, and help-sources.

The four remaining blocks of variables are a summary of those strategies and help-sources that were most and least effective for the women, a summation of the wife's total frequency of use of each strategy or help-source, a set of variables describing the cessation of the violence and summarizing the recommendations and advice that the subjects had for women who are still being battered, and a few variables describing the women's reactions to the promotional strategies of the project. The causal sequencing of all but the last of these blocks of variables is illustrated in figure 2–4.

Data analysis begins with an examination of the frequency distributions for the most important variables and then moves on to correctional analysis and factor analysis. Variables in the study exist at the nominal, ordinal, and interval levels of measurement. To simplify the statistical techniques used

Figure 2–4. Causal Sequencing of Blocks of Variables

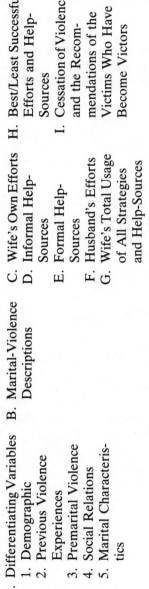

A. Differentiating Variables
   1. Demographic
   2. Previous Violence Experiences
   3. Premarital Violence
   4. Social Relations
   5. Marital Characteristics

B. Marital-Violence Descriptions

C. Wife's Own Efforts

D. Informal Help-Sources

E. Formal Help-Sources

F. Husband's Efforts

G. Wife's Total Usage of All Strategies and Help-Sources

H. Best/Least Successful Efforts and Help-Sources

I. Cessation of Violence and the Recommendations of the Victims Who Have Become Victors and to be as consistent as possible, the categories of nominal variables have been arranged to approximate ordinality where appropriate, and Tau b (an ordinal level correlation measure) has been used to report the strength of bivariate relationships throughout the book. Correlations using multiple response variables were calculated as a check on the representativeness of correlations obtained by using variables derived from the worst and last battering incidents suffered by the women in our study. Since a very high degree of consistency was found among these correlations, the multiple response relationships have not been included in this report.

3

The Dimensions of Violent Marriages and Marital Violence

When the husbands and wives first met, a number of them had already been the victims of violent assaults by their parents, siblings, other family members, friends, acquaintances, and strangers. However, the majority of both husbands and wives in this study had never been exposed to violence previously. This chapter contains findings about the experiences that husbands and wives had with violence before they met, the premarital violence occurring in their relationships, the characteristics of their marital relationships, the nature and extent of the violence suffered by the wives, and the relationships between the dimensions of marital violence and the previous experiences and marital characteristics of the couples.

Wife's Experiences with Violence

Serious disputes occurred frequently in 29 percent of the families of orientation. Thirty-one percent of the wives saw violence between their parents, and, in most of these cases, the violence occurred frequently. The wife observed assaults on her brothers or sisters from one or both of her parents in 22 percent of the cases and was herself assaulted by her parents in 26 percent of the cases. The most common violent experience reported by the wives was being slapped (16 percent by father, 11 percent by mother), with smaller proportions reporting being kicked (10 percent by father, 5 percent by mother), beaten up (3 percent by mother, 5 percent by father) or being threatened or assaulted with a weapon (4 percent by mother, 3 percent by father).

The wives were much more likely to suffer violence from their parents than from any other source. Fourteen of the women were assaulted by a sibling, fourteen by other family members, six by strangers, and five by acquaintances or friends. Considering the violence that was to come, it is surprising how few of these women had experienced violence before they met their future mates. On the other hand, the abuse experienced by those women who suffered assaults in their families of orientation was often severe. In addition to the beatings, six of the women were raped or molested by one or more family members.

Husband's Previous Experiences with Violence

Husbands were exposed to higher levels of violence from all sources than were their wives. Frequent disputes between the husband's parents occurred in nearly half of the families, and 45 percent of the husbands observed violence occurring between their parents. In four out of every five cases in which the husband ever saw violence occurring between the parents, it occurred very often. Similarly, parent-sibling violence occurred in 40 percent of the families, with three-quarters of these families experiencing parent-sibling violence very often. The husband was assaulted by his parents in sixty-two cases (42 percent), and it occurred often in four-fifths of these families. Nineteen of the husbands were assaulted by their brothers or sisters, eight by other family members, thirteen by friends, twenty-three by acquaintances, and thirty-one by strangers. As with other statistics relating to the husbands, these are low estimates, for there were doubtless many cases in which the wives were unaware of the extent of the violence suffered by their husbands prior to their relationships.

Exact details on the violence suffered by the husbands are usually missing due to the wife's limited information. There were a few stereotypically authoritarian fathers who viciously beat their children, and also scattered reports of the use of knives and various implements to assault the husbands.

Premarital Violence

In most of the battering relationships, the wife had little warning of her impending victimization during the dating period. Premarital violence occurred in thirty-nine cases (27 percent of the sample). In most of these relationships, it occurred only once or twice, but there were five cases in which it occurred at least fourteen times. With few exceptions, the premarital violence began more than three months before the couple married. The most common premarital violence was slapping (56 percent of all incidents), followed by pushing, grabbing, or shoving (10 percent), kicking, biting, or punching (8 percent), beating up (5 percent), and threatening the wife with a knife or gun (5 percent). In most of these incidents the future husbands had been drinking or using other psychoactive drugs.

The most common theme found in cases of premarital violence is jealousy. Many of the suitors assumed that their future wives were personal property and became violent whenever the women showed any independence, particularly where that involved contact with other males. The predominant response by the women at the time of the premarital violence was fear (41 percent). Other women were mainly angry (31 percent) or confused (18 percent). Less then a quarter of the women sought help to deal with the premarital violence, and then generally with little success. Most of the women dealt with the problem in isolation and felt unwilling or unable to break off the battering relationship. Almost a third of them were pregnant, a quarter of the women thought that they could change the husband's behavior after marrying, and just under a quarter felt resigned to the violence. In a few cases, the suitors so thoroughly dominated their future wives through violence that the women felt they had to complete marriage plans in order to avoid severe violence and retaliation from their husbands. There was little in the previous experiences of many of these women to aid them in successfully dealing with the unexpected eruption of premarital violence.

In some of the relationships where premarital violence did not occur, the women had a hint of their future husband's propensity for violence through his display of a violent temper. This occurred in approximately one out of every three relationships. The displays of temper were accompanied with violence in some cases. In others, the men were rewarded by increased dominance in the relationship. It is possible that some of these temper outbursts would have proceeded to violence if the future husband had been unable to get his way. A few of the women reacted to the displays of violent temper by learning to suppress their natural reactions, thus avoiding inciting their mates to more extreme displays. The temper outbursts, like the incidents of overt premarital violence, were invariably followed by profuse apologies, which often convinced the women that their husbands' future behavior would be nonviolent.

Characteristics of the Violent Marriages

Couples in the Milwaukee sample were married between 1932 and 1979, with a modal marriage date of 1971. They dated for an average of a year to eighteen months before marrying, and one in every five lived together prior to being married. There were no unusually brief courting periods in the sample, the shortest being six months. The most common reason the women gave for marrying was love (45 percent), followed by pregnancy (26 percent) and social pressure from peers or parents (12 percent).

A third of the women expressed satisfaction with their marital relationship, and twice as many expressed dissatisfaction. Nearly half of the women said that their degree of marital satisfaction had changed over time, with deteriorating satisfaction being the norm. The satisfaction ratings were consistant over different areas of marital life. Thirty-four percent of the women felt that they were very satisfied or fairly satisfied with communication in their marital relationship, 34 percent with their sexual relationship, 34 percent with time spent together, 30 percent with joint participation in specific activities, and 42 percent with affection in their relationship. When asked what was most valued in their marital relationships, 78 percent of the women mentioned children and the same proportion mentioned economic or psychological dependency. Other common marital values were companionship (70 percent), love (66 percent), standard of living (64 percent), common values with the husband (54 percent), and understanding (43 percent). In the opinions of the wives, husbands valued the marital relationship for rather different reasons, including common values (68 percent), love (59 percent), companionship (59 percent), children (50 percent), understanding (48 percent), standard of living (19 percent), and economic or psychological dependency (4 percent). These perceived differences in marital values reflect the economic dependence of many of the women in the sample during the early years of their marriages. Few of them began their marital relationships with the opportunity to earn wages equal to those earned by their husbands.

Separate sets of questions were asked about continuous disagreements in the marital relationship and about sources of high marital stress. The answers to the two sets of questions were so similar that we will take the set of continuous disagreement responses to be indicative of both. Of the twenty areas of disagreements and stress that were discussed, the most commonly mentioned area was financial problems (73 percent), followed by battering (51 percent), chores (49 percent), children (47 percent), drinking or drugs (44 percent), time spent together (40 percent), income (34 percent), and sexual behavior (33 percent). Approximately one quarter of the couples experienced less than four continuous disagreements and sources of stress, and similar proportions experienced (1) four to six disagreements and sources of stress, (2) seven to nine disagreements and sources of stress, and (3) ten or more disagreements and sources of stress. When problems arose between husband and wife, they were settled jointly in approximately half the incidents, but when one member of the marital dyad gave in appreciably more often than the other, the wives saw themselves as much more likely (42 percent) than their husbands (7 percent) to accede to the wishes of their mates.

Nearly three-quarters of the marriages included at least one separation. In a number of cases more than a half-dozen separations occurred. Although the wife was usually the one to leave, the husband left home in approximately a third of the separations. If a woman had children at the time of separation from her husband, she usually took them with her. Most of the women stayed away for at least a week, and one-fourth of them stayed away for at least two months.

These data portray marital relationships that are unsatisfactory from the viewpoint of the battered women. The marital violence was not always perceived as the major source of stress in the relationships. Many other problems existed in the marriages, and most of these appeared to persist after the violence ceased. In some cases where the wife had previously focused on violence as the major marital problem, the solution of this problem helped her realize that the marriage had many other problems. In still another pattern of human growth and development, some of the women were so changed by having overcome the violence that they were no longer willing to continue in relationships that previously had been acceptable to them. The terms on which they were willing to accept a permanent partner had now become more equalitarian.

Social Embedment

Are some husbands able to assault their wives with impunity because their families' isolation from the surrounding community reduces the social controls that would minimize or eliminate these assaults? Or in a patriarchal society such as ours, is the support of a husband's domination of his wife greater, even if that entails violence, the more a family is integrated within a community? To evaluate questions such as these, information was collected on the social relations of each husband and wife with friends and relatives, as well as their participation in recreational organizations and their pattern of residency. Little evidence of social isolation was found in this sample of violent families. The modal number of times moved during the marital relationship was 3.5 (mean = 5.2), and two-thirds of the couples owned a home rather than rented one. The average date of purchase for the most recently owned homes was 1970.

The wives were not more socially isolated than their husbands; on the contrary, they were significantly less isolated on a number of dimensions. Wives were more likely than husbands to have close relationships with relatives (68 percent of wives, compared with 53 percent of husbands), and much more likely to have enjoyed close relationships with these relatives since childhood (67 percent of the wives and 40 percent of the husbands had ever had close relationships with relatives). The women were also more likely than their husbands to have close personal friends (86 percent to 66 percent). The wives were involved with an average of 3.0 recreational organizations as compared to 2.4 for the husbands. Most commonly, women participated in educational classes (36 percent) and church-sponsored activities (30 percent), while the men were more likely to participate in sports activities (25 percent) and educational classes (18 percent).

Although these data establish the fact that couples in our sample were not unusually isolated, they cannot determine the relationship between social embedment and marital violence because the study lacks a control group of nonviolent families. We will see how social embedment variables relate to the severity of violence among violent families in a later section of this chapter. The summary descriptions previously provided allow us to conclude that it is possible for severe marital violence to exist over long periods of time in families that are not unusually isolated from friends, relatives, and other socially integrating aspects of their communities.

Nature and Extent of Wife-Beating

The first beating suffered by the women occurred an average of thirteen years before the interview. Alcohol was involved in half of the first incidents, with the modal number of drinks being seven or eight. The children were assaulted in five of the first incidents, marital rape was part of the assault in eight of these incidents, and two miscarriages occurred as a result of the initial assaults. As time went on, the children were increasingly likely to be assaulted (for example, in 28 percent of the worst battering incidents), and marital rape also became more common (12 percent of the worst incidents, 14 percent of the last incidents). The use of intoxicants (overwhelmingly alcohol) increased slightly, peaking at 63 percent in the worst incidents, and the level of intoxication was steady at seven to eight drinks. There were one or two miscarriages among the 146 women in each of the first, second, third, worst, and last incidents.

Table 3–1 presents the distribution of the most severe violence suffered in each of the five specific battering incidents included in the study. The category including hitting, slapping, kicking, biting, and punching comprises the violence used in the majority of all battering incidents except the worst; in the worst incidents this category of violence was still more common than any other. The more severe violent categories—"beat up" and "threatened with or used weapons"—were approximately three times as common in the worst incident as in the first incident. There were only a few cases in which the final incident was also the worst incident.

Table 3–1
Most Severe Violence in Five Incidents
(percentage)

Most Severe. Violence	Battering Incident				
	First	Second	Third	Worst	Last
Threw object	17	11	4	1	7
Hit, slapped, kicked, bit, punched	63	71	64	43	54
Beat up	13	9	21	35	23
Threatened with or used weapons	7	9	11	21	16
Total	100	100	100	100	100

N = 146

A quarter of the subjects suffered no more than ten beatings, a quarter suffered between eleven and forty beatings, and the remaining half of the subjects suffered more than forty beatings in their marital relationships. Children were involved in at least one of the beatings suffered by 54 percent of the women. Fifty-six percent were beaten at least once while pregnant (the average being 4.5 beatings while pregnant for each of these women). Ten of the women suffered miscarriages as a result of the beatings, and thirty-three (23 percent) were maritally raped, most of them numerous times.

To protect the identities of the subjects, no identifying details of their characteristics or experiences are presented here. Before going on to the statistical analysis of patterns of violence and their correlates, a series of themes summarizing situations that were commonly experienced by many of the women in the sample are presented. These themes are categorized under three headings: (1) dimensions of the violence, (2) patterns of the violence, and (3) termination of violence.

Dimensions of Violence

1. A common theme was the extensiveness of the violence. Many of the women suffered violent incidents weekly or even three or four times a week over a period of many years; in some cases for more than a decade.

2. Jealousy was the most common theme in the violent incidents. Many of the husbands did not want their wives to be close to anyone except themselves. They were jealous of other men and sometimes of other women or of their own children. The jealousy often led to uncontrollable rage and then to physical assault of the women.

3. Sexual perversion and rape were important components of the abuse in some of the relationships. Sexual perversion is taken to mean sexual acts that the women considered distasteful but felt compelled to perform. Marital rape includes sexual perversion as well as the more standard sexual acts forced upon the women. Rape is distinguished by the use of overt physical aggression instead of or in addition to verbal manipulation to compel the women to participate against their wills. The frequency of marital rape would have been much higher had it not been for the fact that some of the women were sometimes so badly beaten prior to having sex that they were no longer able to resist their husband's demands.

4. Some of the husbands took great care to keep the battering a secret. These men avoided hitting their wives in the company of others; they used techniques that would render no visible bruises; and they assaulted their wives only when their children were asleep. Even when drunk, these men were careful to avoid public demonstrations of their assaultiveness.

5. Some of the husbands were not content to beat their wives. They

systematically resorted to alternative abusive techniques, such as cutting their wives' hair, burning them with cigarettes, locking them up, and using particularly painful weapons in the beatings.

6. As a correlate of the physical battering, most of the husbands were psychologically abusive to their wives. Some of them wrote threatening notes to their wives, and others teased them constantly about their weaknesses, tortured them with their intimate knowledge about their phobias, killed their pets, and otherwise caused them mental anguish.

7. Next to jealousy, the most common theme expressed by the women was the use of alcohol in connection with the violence. Many of the husbands were heavy drinkers, but most who beat their wives when drunk also occasionally beat them when sober.

8. The children in these violent families suffered a high risk of involvement in the battering incidents. They were also in danger of being beaten separately by their fathers. In this theme, the patriarchal head of the household assaulted anyone who dared to challenge his authority.

Patterns of Violence

1. The husband begins the argument and the wife is goaded into joining in. Once she is heavily involved in the argument, it escalates to the level of overt violence.

2. There is a general argument between husband and wife that grows in stages from an area of continuous disagreement, such as finances or the children. At some point, the husband becomes enraged and begins to beat the wife.

3. The wife confronts the husband about some undesirable aspect of his behavior, or inadequacy of his performance on behalf of the family, and he responds with violence rather than reasonable discussion about the problem.

4. The husband has suffered a humiliation at work or with his friends or relatives, and he responds by taking it out on his wife when he gets home. This exemplifies the kick-the-cat theory of the displacement of aggression.

5. The husband engages in overt violence against his wife only after drinking. This does not necessarily imply the absence of volition in the husband's violence, for he may deliberately drink to facilitate a violent encounter.

6. The wife gives attention to the children, or goes out with friends, or is friendly to another man, and the husband becomes uncontrollably jealous. The fight begins with verbal abuse and soon escalates to violence, sometimes not until he children are in bed.

7. With some husbands, the violence appears to be cyclical, and women can predict when the next episode might occur almost to the day. However, there was no common cycle length associated with the violence reported by the Milwaukee subjects. Different men apparently had different cycles. Unfortunately, the available evidence does not permit going beyond this simple observation about the cyclical pattern of male violence.

Termination of a Violent Incident

1. A common theme suggested that the husband was assaultive until he was exhausted. The wife was, in essense, a punching bag, and when the husband reached catharsis the violence ceased. A second way in which an incident came to an end was when the wife gave in totally, becoming limp; a human analog of the gesture of baring the throat that is found among some species of animals.

2. In some cases, the violence ended because the children directly intervened and were able to get the batterer to desist. Alternatively, the wife may have been able to instill a sense of guilt for involving the children or over the possibility that they might overhear the battering.

3. Many violent incidents terminated because the wife threatened to call the police or to get a divorce. Other episodes ended when the police were summoned to the scene of the crime.

4. There were numerous cases in which the wives physically resisted the aggressors. In many of these cases, their husbands responded with an increase in the severity of the violence. In other cases, the wives' willingness to fight back, or their threatening to kill the aggressor once he was asleep or off guard was sufficient to end the incident. However, counterviolence was found to be a dangerous strategy, because when it was unsuccessful there was a significant possibility of increased injury to the wives.

Relationship between Demographic Characteristics and Marital Violence

In table 3-2 and the following tables, a standard set of seven variables is used to encompass the quantifiable aspects of marital violence experienced by the women in the study. The seven characteristics are

1. Frequency of violence over the entire period of the battering relationship
2. Violence carried out against the children

Table 3–2
Relationships between Demographic and Marital Violence Characteristics

Demographic Characteristics	Marital Violence Characteristics						
	Frequency	Children Assaulted	Chemicals in Worst Incident	When Pregnant	Marital Rape	Most Severe Violence	Years of Violence
Wife							
Parental income	-.07	-.07	-.02	-.19	.05	-.09	.14
Mother's occupation	-.08	-.07	-.05	-.17	-.02	-.14	-.08
Occupation	-.02	-.07	-.06	.01	-.06	-.02	-.01
Education	-.19	-.16	-.03	-.15	-.11	-.04	-.08
Religion	.03	.14	.05	.02	.08	.01	.08
Religiosity	-.05	.11	-.02	.04	.00	.05	.14
Age	-.05	.18	.29	-.03	-.11	-.16	.56
Current income	-.19	-.05	-.03	-.21	-.18	-.21	.14
Current marital status	-.19	.07	-.17	.08	-.26	-.23	.12
Husband							
Parental income	.11	-.10	-.08	-.15	-.15	.11	-.26
Mother's occupation	-.21	-.06	-.25	-.14	-.09	.17	-.09
Occupation	-.15	.01	-.02	-.12	-.06	-.05	-.01
Education	-.18	-.12	-.09	-.10	-.13	-.10	-.02
Religion	.06	.02	.00	.10	.01	.08	.02
Religiosity	-.11	.05	-.02	-.06	-.13	-.14	-.21
Age	-.05	.17	.18	-.11	-.07	-.16	.51
Armed forces	.02	.20	.14	.02	-.05	.03	.10
Together							
Year of marriage	-.09	-.21	-.25	-.13	-.03	.08	-.69
Number of children	.17	.31	.20	.23	.04	-.10	.48
Parental income dissimilarity	.06	-.11	.08	.02	-.05	-.09	.08
Occupational dissimilarity	.05	.05	.07	-.02	.08	.04	-.01
Age dissimilarity	-.05	.05	.05	.11	-.07	.03	.05
Religion dissimilarity	.01	-.04	.01	.00	-.09	.06	-.16
Recreational organization dissimilarity	.15	-.03	.18	.01	.13	-.08	-.06

N = 146; all correlations are Tau b

3. Chemicals (alcohol or other psychoactive drugs) used in the worst battering incident
4. Violence carried out against the woman when she was pregnant
5. Marital rape
6. The severity of the violence carried out against the wife in the worst battering incident
7. The total span of years over which violence occurred in the relationship

Table 3–2 presents Tau b correlations between the seven marital violence characteristics and a selection of two dozen of the most interesting demographic characteristics of the wife, the husband, and the pair. The correlations between demographic characteristics and dimensions of marital violence are generally low. The most influential demographic characteristics are the wife's education, age, current income, current marital status, the occupation of the husband's mother, his age, the year in which the couple was married, and their number of children.

Women with higher levels of education tended to suffer less severe violence on all seven dimensions. The age of the wife was naturally correlated with the number of years of violence suffered, since older women have been at risk for more years than younger women. The concept of time at risk also explains much of the size of the correlation between age and assaults against children, but it does not explain why older women were more likely to be assaulted by mates under the influence of alcohol or drugs, or why they suffered less severe violence than younger women in the worst battering incident. It appears that there are two contrasting forces producing these correlations. On one hand, women who are older have been married longer, and therefore have been exposed to the possibility of battering over a much longer period of time. On the other hand, there appears to be a trend toward increasing severity of violence against women in the Milwaukee sample. It was difficult to separate the effects of age or year married from length of marriage for two reasons: sample size was small, and there were too few women in the sample who had been married for only a few years and whose marriages occurred more than a decade ago. This same interpretation applies to the correlations found between dimensions of marital violence and both husband's age and year of marriage.

Husbands whose mothers had never worked outside of the home beat their wives more frequently and were more likely to drink heavily in connection with the batterings, but their batterings tended to be somewhat less severe than those administered by men whose mothers had worked outside the home. The greater the number of children in the family of procreation, the worse the violence was likely to be, as measured by frequency, assaults on children, involvement of alcohol and other drugs, violence when pregnant, and total years of violence. These correlations are partially a function of the length of the marriage and show additional at-risk components in that (1) children were more likely to be assaulted in homes with many children than in homes with few children, and (2) wives who had been pregnant many times were more likely to be assaulted when pregnant than wives who had been pregnant only a few times.

Women with higher current incomes were less likely than women with lower current incomes to have been beaten while pregnant or to have suffered marital rape, and they experienced less severe beatings. They also suffered somewhat longer periods of violence, but that is primarily because they were older than women at lower income levels. Although the women who eventually left their husbands had forced them to end the battering and thus solved the problem of marital violence, the characteristics of the violence against them were not unrelated to their decision to leave. The frequency of the violence, the involvement of alcohol and other drugs with the violence, marital rape, and the severity of the beatings all tended to increase the chances that a woman would eventually leave her husband.

Table 3–2 is more important for the weak correlations than for those which are strong. The lack of strong correlations is inconsistent with five theoretical notions about wife-beating. The first notion is that wife-beating is more frequent and severe in the lower classes than in the middle and upper classes. Social class was indexed primarily by parental income and current occupation for both husband and wife, and few of twenty-eight correlations between these variables and marital violence characteristics were much different from zero. In the Milwaukee sample, there was essentially no relationship between social class and the dimensions of marital violence. However, because of the unstructured way in which the sample was recruited, these findings cannot be taken to be a serious challenge to existing wisdom on the relationship between social class and marital violence. Only a random sample permits a definitive answer to epidemiological questions such as this one.

There were also few indications of support for a second notion, that the husband's experiences in the armed forces predisposed him toward marital violence. It makes sense to assume that men who were trained in the techniques of violence in the armed forces would be predisposed to beat their wives more severely and extensively than those who were not so trained. It might also be assumed that their frequent viewing of violence in the armed forces would tend to desensitize them to the horror of violence. These assumptions are not supported by our data.

The third notion is that husbands whose mothers did not work outside the home are more paternalistic than those whose mothers had outside jobs, and that this paternalism leads to greater severity of violence. Although three of seven correlations between the occupation of the husband's mother and the dimensions of marital violence are above $\pm$ .15, only two of the three correlations are in the expected direction. These correlations offer little support for a connection between wife-beating and paternalism in the husband's family of orientation. The correlations between the occupation of the wife's mother and violence characteristics are remarkably close to zero, indicating no effect whatever of paternalism in the wife's family of orientation on the characteristics of her own marital victimization.

It is commonly said that "the family that prays together, stays together." A fourth notion is derived from this statement, suggesting that families high in religiosity have markedly lower values for the marital violence characteristics. None of the seven correlations involving wife's frequency of church attendance and only one of the correlations involving husband's frequency of church attendance is above $\pm$ .15. For the families in the Milwaukee sample, it appears that frequent church attendance by the husband tended to shorten the total length of the violence and to decrease its severity slightly, but it had no effect on the frequency of the assaults, the involvement of children in the beatings, the use of alcohol or other drugs during the abuse, violence when pregnant, or marital rape. There is also little evidence to support the opposite theoretical notion that the church acts as an agent of paternalism and, therefore, may be associated with increased rather than decreased marital violence. The single supportive evidence for this notion is that there was a slight tendency for women who attended church often to suffer more years of violence than women who attended church infrequently or not at all.

The threat theory of marital violence suggests a fifth notion. Women who have higher socioeconomic status than their husbands may have a particularly high risk of being beaten as their husbands attempt to establish paternalistic control of the family without their usual status and income advantages. It is not possible to say whether marital violence is more likely to occur in such families than in those in which the husband is able to dominate through his control of income and similar social and economic factors. However, it can be reported that the severity of violence experienced by the subjects in the Milwaukee study was no greater for the women having higher status than their husbands than for those with lower status. Indexes of spousal dissimilarity were computed by subtracting the husband's demographic characteristics from the wife's demographic characteristics on a number of variables. Each index was then correlated with the set of marital violence dimensions. All of the correlations with parental income dissimilarity, occupational dissimilarity, and even age dissimilarity cluster near zero. Dissimilarity in religion, which is not an index of differential status, is related mainly to total years of violence; and dissimilarity in the number of recreational organizations is primarily related to the frequency of violence and the involvement of alcohol and other drugs. The Milwaukee data clearly do not support the notion that higher socioeconomic status on the part of the wife leads to increased severity of marital violence.

Influence of Previous Experiences with Violence on the Dimensions of Marital Violence

Are women who have suffered violence in their earlier lives more likely than other women in the sample to suffer severe violence in the battering relationship? Are husbands who have previously been the victims of violence more likely than other battering husbands to severely beat their wives? Can the severity of the marital beatings be predicted from the characteristics of premarital violence? These questions are answered in table 3–3.

It is evident that the wife's previous experiences with parental disputes, seeing parental assaults and being assaulted by parents, has essentially no relationship to the characteristics of her own marital victimization. (Of course, the study does not deal with the question of whether previous experience with violence is a predictor of violence in the wife's marriage.) Six of the twenty-one relationships involving (1) the husband's experience of parental disputes, (2) seeing parental assaults, and (3) being assaulted by parents are above $\pm$ .15, all in the expected direction. Assaults on the husband by strangers are not related to any of marital violence dimensions at $\pm$ .15 or above. There is no evidence here to support the idea that battered women who experienced violence in their families of orientation were willing to accept more violence from their husbands than battered women who had no previous experience with violence. The tendency for husbands with previous violence experience to assault their wives more frequently, particularly when they were pregnant, is suggestive, but hardly conclusive. For example, not one of the correlations between the husband's previous experiences with violence and the severity of his abusive activities reaches $\pm$ .10.

Three indicators of marital violence potential were selected from the premarital experiences of the women. These are: (1) a woman suspected that her future husband had a violent temper, (2) he beat her when they were dating, (3) alcohol or other psychoactive drugs were involved in the beatings. The presence of alcohol or other psychoactive drugs is the strongest predictor of the characteristics of later marital violence, correlating .44 with the frequency of violence, .75 with the use of alcohol or psychoactive drugs in the worst incident, .30 with assault while pregnant, and .27 with total years of violence. Suspicions of a violent temper were directly related to the use of alcohol and drugs and to violence when pregnant, but inversely related to the total years of violence. The frequency of premarital violence was directly related to the frequency of marital violence, yet inversely

Table 3–3
Relationships between Previous Experiences with Violence and Marital Violence Characteristics

Previous Experiences with Violence	Marital Violence Characteristics						
	Frequency	Children Assaulted	Chemicals in Worst Incident	When Pregnant	Marital Rape	Most Severe Violence	Years of Violence
Wife							
Frequency of parental disputes	.06	-.12	-.03	.09	.09	-.07	.05
Saw parental assaults	.07	-.06	-.04	.11	.10	-.05	-.13
Assaulted by parents	.01	-.02	-.05	.02	-.01	-.01	-.17
Husband							
Frequency of parental disputes	.19	-.03	.08	.32	.07	.02	.13
Saw parental assaults	.16	.12	-.05	.14	.24	.02	.13
Assaulted by parents	.21	.09	.03	.20	.07	-.08	.00
Assaulted by strangers	.08	.08	.02	.14	.08	-.04	-.11
Together—Premarital							
Wife suspected violent temper	.10	-.10	.17	.16	.04	.12	-.16
Frequency of pre-marital violence	.15	-.09	.12	.13	.05	.12	-.25
Alcohol/drugs involved	.44	.01	.75	.30	-.08	-.20	.27

N = 146; all correlations are Tau b

related to the total years of violence. Although many of the women in the sample sensed the propensity of their husbands for violence before they were married, the only factor consistently related to most of the characteristics of marital violence was the use of alcohol or other psychoactive drugs.

Effect of Social Embedment on Marital Violence Characteristics

Social control occurs more often through informal social relationships, such as those associated with the family, friends, and recreational activities, than through the formal activities of the criminal-justice system. It is reasonable to assume that the strength of informal social control varies directly with the frequency of contacts with family, friends, and additional significant others, and also with the closeness of the relationships with these individuals. If a society severely disapproves of marital violence, we might expect the marital violence characteristics to be inversely related to indices of the social relationships of the wife and husband with family members and other individuals in the community. These statistical relationships are summarized under the heading of social embedment.

Table 3–4 convinces us that the wife's social embedment, as indexed by her contact with parents, contact with in-laws, closeness to relatives, contact with friends, and participation in recreational organizations, is irrelevant to the characteristics of the marital violence that she has suffered. The social embedment of the husband is somewhat more important, mainly in relation to his friends. Five of seven relationships involving the husband's contact with friends are above ± .15. In addition, one of seven relationships with participation in recreational organizations and one relationship with his closeness to relatives are above the ± .15 standard. The interesting thing about these relationships is that all correlations over .15 are positive, indicating that increased social embedment leads to greater seriousness of violence, as indicated by increased violence frequency, assaults on the children, use of alcohol and psychoactive drugs, violence when wife's pregnant, and severity of violence in the worst incident. These correlations point to the possibility of a male peer subculture of violence that justifies wife-beating, and strongly suggests that the better integrated the battering husband is into this peer subculture, the more severely he is likely to beat his wife.

Another series of dimensions indexing social embedment are time at the current address, the number of times moved during the relationship, and home ownership. These dimensions tell us something about the geographical stability of the families in the Milwaukee study. It is assumed that high geographical mobility reduces informal social controls by reducing

Table 3–4
Relationships between Social Embedment Variables and Marital Violence Characteristics

Social Embedment Variables	Marital Violence Characteristics						
	Frequency	Children Assaulted	Chemicals in Worst Incident	When Pregnant	Marital Rape	Most Severe Violence	Years of Violence
Wife							
Contact with parents	-.04	-.08	-.10	.01	-.02	.01	-.01
Contact with in-laws	.04	.00	.02	-.03	.08	-.02	.00
Close to relatives	-.04	-.01	.16	-.06	-.06	-.05	-.05
Contact with friends	-.08	.07	.07	-.12	-.10	.06	.11
Number of recreational organizations	-.07	.01	.08	.05	-.09	-.16	.11
Husband							
Contact with parents	.10	-.03	.01	.00	.07	-.01	.00
Contact with in-laws	-.04	-.12	-.06	.02	-.04	-.03	-.04
Close to relatives	.15	.09	-.02	.05	-.03	-.01	.03
Contact with friends	.17	.19	.17	.19	.03	.39	.12
Number of recreational organizations	-.14	-.02	-.07	.04	-.12	-.03	.26
Together—Premarital							
Time at current address	-.01	.09	.22	-.04	-.11	-.14	-.41
Times moved	.23	.11	-.09	.32	.02	.10	.19
Home ownership	-.06	.07	.15	-.04	-.04	-.23	.43

N = 146; all correlations are Tau b

social embedment. Similarily, social embedment may be assumed to be directly related to time at the current address and to home ownership. The longer a family stays in a given residence, the more likely family members are to develop close relationships with neighbors and to care about the neighbors' attitudes toward their marital behavior. Eight of the twenty-one correlations between geographical variables and marital violence character-istics are at ± .15 or more; half of them in the expected direction, and half in the opposite direction. The relationships that are not in the expected direc-tion appear to be largely conditioned by associations between the geograph-ical variables and the length of the marital relationship, thus failing to undermine the embedment theory. The correlations that are in the expected direction indicate that frequent moves are associated with increased fre-quency of assaults, wife-beating when she's pregnant, and total years of violence; and that home ownership depresses the severity of violence in the worst incident.

Relationships between Marital Characteristics and Marital Violence

Wife-beating is not independent of other dimensions of marital relation-ships. In table 3–5, we see that the frequency of the batterings, marital rape, and the severity of violence in the worst incident are consistently related to the wife's marital satisfaction and to continuous disagreements between husband and wife. The wife's marital values are related to the frequency of battering, assaults on children, violence when pregnant, and the severity of violence in the worst incident. The husband's marital values are much less likely to be related to marital violence characteristics, with violence when pregnant and the severity of violence in the worst incident being the most sensitive to his marital values. There are few correlations above ± .15 between the series of marital value dissimilarity indexes, which were constructed to measure the differences in marital values between wife and husband, and the dimensions of marital violence.

Without exception, battering relationships with high frequencies of assaults, high violence severity, and marital rape are associated with low marital satisfaction by the wife. However, there is some indication that marital satisfaction is higher where alcohol and psychoactive drugs are part of the violence pattern than where these chemicals are not. Relationships between continuous marital disagreements and marital violence characteris-tics tend to show that the more serious the disagreements, the more serious the violence. Women who placed a high value on children in the marriage were more likely than the other battered wives to be assaulted frequently, to have their children assaulted, to have chemicals involved in the violence, to be beaten when pregnant, and to have suffered violence over a long period of time; but they were less likely to suffer marital rape or severe violence in

Table 3–5
Relationships between Marital and Marital Violence Characteristics

Marital Characteristics	Marital Violence Characteristics						
	Frequency	Children Assaulted	Chemicals in Worst Incident	When Pregnant	Marital Rape	Most Severe Violence	Years of Violence
Wife's Marital Satisfaction							
Satisfaction overall	−.20	−.08	.20	−.11	−.29	−.35	.06
Quality of Communication	−.18	−.12	.09	−.06	−.29	−.33	.08
Affection	−.20	−.09	.15	−.14	−.33	−.20	.02
Sex	−.24	−.13	.17	−.13	−.36	−.23	.00
Time together	−.23	−.08	.12	−.11	−.24	−.35	.09
Tried to do joint activities	−.20	−.15	.10	−.11	−.17	−.35	.19
Satisfaction with joint activities	−.20	−.14	.10	−.06	−.23	−.31	.10
Continuous Disagreements							
Total continuous disagreements	.16	.16	.11	.08	.26	.24	−.04
Finances	.06	.13	−.02	.00	.30	.18	.02
Friends	.14	.08	−.08	.19	.18	.10	.01
Children	.04	.27	−.14	.04	.15	.10	.01
Drinking/drugs	.22	.09	.28	.00	.31	.16	−.07
Battering	.28	.08	−.07	.05	.34	.34	−.14
Reason for Marriage	−.23	−.07	−.05	−.14	−.11	−.15	.00
Frequency of Separations	.19	.13	−.04	.18	.10	.18	−.05
Problem Resolution							
Recent	−.05	.09	.03	−.09	.04	.17	−.05
Earlier	.03	−.07	.04	.04	.17	−.06	−.03
Wife's Marital Values							
Children	.19	.22	.16	.22	−.15	−.15	.33
Standard of living	.01	−.02	.18	−.11	−.11	−.24	.05
Understanding	−.21	−.23	.07	−.13	−.07	−.30	.07

Table 3–5 *(continued)*

Love	-.18	-.22	.03	-.13	-.03	-.16	-.03
Companionship	-.12	-.17	.15	.15	-.04	-.24	.02
Common values	-.19	-.13	.19	-.30	.00	.12	-.01
Dependency	.22	.07	.11	.14	.12	-.04	.10
Husband's Marital Values							
Children	-.03	-.06	.20	.11	-.21	-.04	.25
Standard of living	-.06	.11	-.01	-.11	.04	-.06	.07
Understanding	-.20	-.01	.05	-.21	-.19	-.23	.09
Love	-.13	-.29	.04	-.17	-.01	-.26	-.01
Companionship	-.13	-.11	.16	-.25	.00	-.22	.07
Common values	.07	-.03	.06	.00	.02	-.17	.03
Dependency	-.10	-.01	.08	.15	-.13	.07	.20
Marital-Value Dissimilarity							
Total	.02	-.07	-.01	.02	.05	-.16	-.02
Children	.21	.27	.03	.01	.19	.05	-.07
Standard of living	.12	-.07	-.05	-.08	.03	-.08	-.03
Understanding	.07	.07	.12	-.09	.15	.13	-.16
Love	.05	-.02	.04	.08	-.01	.00	-.05
Companionship	-.02	-.07	-.25	.09	-.02	-.03	-.05
Common values	.11	.16	-.26	.28	.05	.06	.06
Dependency	.27	.00	-.02	.12	.28	-.06	.03

N = 146; all correlations are Tau b

the worst battering incident. If they placed a high value on understanding between themselves and their husbands, they were less likely to suffer frequent violence, to have their children assaulted, to be battered when pregnant, or to suffer extremely severe violence in the worst battering incident.

The husband's values that were most important in predicting the seriousness of violence were understanding, love, and companionship, with all of these values being inversely related to beating a pregnant wife and the severity of violence in the worst incident. Of course, the accuracy of the data on the husband's values cannot be considered to be as high as the accuracy of data on the wife's values, since the husband's values were almost entirely reported by the wives rather than directly by the husbands. The wives' perceptions of their husbands' values may have been distorted by the severity of the violence suffered at the hands of their mates.

It was expected that value dissimilarity between husband and wife might be a major determinant of the seriousness of marital violence because it would presumably lead to the kinds of arguments that often escalated to overt violence. This was not generally found to be the case. The most important area of marital value dissimilarity was children. Marriages in which the wife and husband placed different values on children tended to be higher in frequency of battering, assaults on children, and marital rape; but there were no substantial differences on the other marital violence characteristics. Value disimilarity with respect to economic or psychological dependency was associated with increased frequency of violence and marital rape. Despite these suggestive findings, the overall effect of marital value dissimilarity on violence characteristics is small in the Milwaukee sample.

Three other marital characteristics included in the Milwaukee study are (1) the most important reason for getting married, (2) the frequency of separations in the marriage, and (3) the power balance in the marriage. Women who married because they were pregnant suffered higher frequencies of violence, greater severity of violence in the worst incident, and a higher probability of violence when pregnant than the other wives. The frequency of violence, assaults on children, violence when pregnant, and severity of violence in the worst incident were associated with the number of separations. There were few indications of a relationship between the husband's dominance of the marriage (as indexed by marital problem resolution) and any of the marital violence characteristics, either in the period during which the batterings occurred or afterward.

Analysis of Marital Violence Characteristics

One might ask to what extent seriousness of violence on one dimension is related to seriousness of violence on another dimension. Table 3–6 presents the intercorrelations among the marital violence characteristics. The corre-

Table 3–6
Intercorrelations among Marital Violence Characteristics

	Frequency	Children Assaulted	Chemicals in Worst Incident	When Pregnant	Marital Rape	Most Severe Violence	Years of Violence
Frequency							
Children assaulted	.21						
Chemicals in worst incident	-.12	-.05					
When pregnant	.44	.16	-.04				
Marital rape	.20	.03	.06	.07			
Most severe violence	.25	.24	-.03	.15	.10		
Years of violence	.06	.18	.14	.23	.04	-.15	

N = 146; all correlations are Tau b

lations are suprisingly low, with only ten of twenty-one correlations reaching ± .15. The highest correlation is between the frequency of violence and violence to pregnant wife. All of the correlations are in the expected direction, except one in which there is an inverse relationship between total years of violence and the severity of violence in the worst incident.

A careful inspection of the bivariate relationships between the marital violence characteristics produced no clear typology of violence types. The set of seven marital violence characteristics were then subjected to a factor analysis which yielded two factors. The rotated factor matrix is presented in table 3–7. By far the strongest variable in factor one is violence frequency, and factor two is dominated by total years of violence. It was therefore determined to simplify the data by developing a typology around these two variables rather than using factor score coefficients to build complex factor variables. Table 3–8 displays the bivariate relationship between the frequency of marital violence and the total years of marital violence, and table 3–9 rearranges these data into a simple marital violence typology formed by the intersection of these two variables, each being dichotomized into high and low values. Twenty-one percent of the women in the sample suffered the least-serious marital violence, 18 percent suffered the most-serious marital violence, and 61 percent suffered marital violence of intermediate seriousness. It should be remembered that these marital violence ratings are comparative only with respect to the women in the study, not with respect to marital violence in general.

Few of the correlations between this newly created violence variable and the demographic variables, social embedment variables, previous violence experiences of husband and wife, and characteristics of their marital relationships reached ± .15. The strongest relationships were with wife's age (Tau b = .41), husband's age (Tau b = .37), number of children (Tau b = .25), home ownership (Tau b = .23), time at the current address (Tau b = .30), year of marriage (Tau b = −.50), and the use of alcohol or other psychoactive drugs in the worst battering incident (Tau b = .34).

Table 3–7
Factor Analysis of Marital Violence Characteristics

Marital Violence Characteristics	Factor 1	Factor 2
Rotated Factor Matrix		
Violence frequency	.723	.175
Children assaulted	.340	.125
Chemicals in worst incident	.058	.241
When pregnant	.476	.334
Marital rape	.218	.032
Most severe violence	.534	−.285
Years of violence	.049	.700

N = 146

Table 3–8
Relationship between Frequency and Total Years of
Marital Violence

Marital Violence	Total Years of Marital Violence[a]			
Frequency	0–5	6–10	11–15	Over 15
1–10 times	30	34	6	25
11–40 times	25	16	35	25
Over 40 times	46	50	59	50
Total percent	101	100	100	100
N	57	38	17	32

[a]Percentages may not sum 100 due to rounding.

Table 3–9
Simple Marital Violence Typology

Marital Violence Dimensions	Number of Cases	Percentage
Least serious marital violence		
1. Low frequency of violence; low total years of violence	30	21
Mixed types		
2. High frequency of violence; low total years of violence	45	31
3. Low frequency of violence; high total years of violence	43	30
Most serious marital violence		
4. High frequency of violence; high total years of violence	26	18
Total	144	100

N = 144

4

Personal Strategies and Techniques Used by Battered Wives

There are three groups of forces that battered wives can bring to bear on their husbands to end marital violence. These are their own personal strategies and techniques, informal help-sources, and formal help-sources. Chapter 4 deals with the first of these three groups of forces. Chapter 5 presents material on informal help-sources, and chapter 6 details parallel material on formal help-sources.

Six personal strategies were originally identified by the project: (1) talking the man out of the abuse, (2) finding a way to have him promise to end the abuse, (3) threatening him with some sort of nonviolent action, such as contacting the police or filing for a divorce, (4) hiding from him, (5) using passive self-defense during the beatings to minimize the physical damage incurred, and (6) relying on aggressive defense during the beatings by fighting back against the aggressor. A seventh category, avoidance, was initially considered to be a nonstrategy, and so a less complete set of data was collected here. In retrospect, the way in which avoidance was used by the women does constitute a seventh strategy; one that is different from hiding in that it occurs before the beginning of overt aggression rather than after the battering has begun.

The personal strategies outlined above are analytically distinct, but they overlap in practice. This is not just a matter of the wives using more than a single strategy in each incident. The boundaries between talking and promising, as well as between some of the other combinations of strategies, are not always clear as the battering incidents unfold. Reconstructed reality as portrayed by social scientists is always an oversimplification of social reality as experienced by the actors in specific settings.

Talking

Data were collected on 283 incidents in which the wives attempted to talk their husbands out of continuing the abuse. The talking-strategy consisted mainly of using rational arguments to convince the husband to cease his abuse. This technique comprised 91 percent of all uses of the talking-strategy. The only other technique occurring in more than two or three cases was working with the husband to rationalize his behavior in terms of his problems with alcohol or drugs. This occurred in 5 percent of the cases. The strategy of talking was used in 33 percent of all the incidents on which data were collected. Table 4–1 shows that there was little variation in the use of the talking-strategy from the first to the last incident. Here is an example of the use of talking.

> John and Lorraine always had good communication in their marriage. However, she had no luck in talking him out of a beating once it had begun because he seemed to become temporarily insane when enraged. She kept after him between incidents, trying to get him to admit that he was wrong and to promise to stop beating her. He eventually agreed to the idea that a good marriage should be violence-free, but claimed that her constant yelling drove him mad. They finally reached a compromise in which Lorraine agreed not to yell at John, and he agreed to try to refrain from assaulting her.

In some cases, talking was a matter of a brief discussion, while for others, it was a continuous dialogue that dominated the marriage over a period of many years. It was impossible to discuss the problem with some of the husbands because they became irrational during the violent incidents, as well as whenever the beatings were brought up for discussion. Other men insisted on blaming alcohol for the violence, or used a homespun psychological analysis to justify their assaultive behavior because they were threatened by their wives. Still others made clear that they would be happy to end the abuse if their wives conceded all independence and obeyed their husbands without question. The wives who were most successful with the talking-strategy were those who kept calm and rational, showed little fear of their husbands (although they may have felt much), and embarrassed their mates by confronting them with the results of their actions (for example, by displaying their bruises prominently). The battered wives rated the talking-technique as fairly successful in 32 percent of the cases in which it was used, neither successful nor unsuccessful in 39 percent, fairly unsuccessful in 28 percent, and very unsuccessful in 1 percent. Successfulness in this context means reducing the level of violence or terminating it in the current incident,

Table 4–1
Proportion of Wives using Personal Strategies in Five Incidents
(percentage)

Personal Strategies	Battering Incident				
	First	*Second*	*Third*	*Worst*	*Last*
Talk	35	38	32	30	34
Promise	43	42	46	52	44
Threaten	10	10	22	30	38
Hide	19	22	32	26	22
Passive defense	89	90	92	90	90
Aggressive defense	18	29	25	39	28
Avoidance	42	44	52	55	51

N=146

or contributing to the eventual permanent cessation of the abuse. Usefulness might be a better term for the purpose of description, but successfulness has been retained because it was the term used in the interviews with the battered wives.

Promising

The promising-strategy was used in 45 percent of the incidents. The arguments leading to promises to end the violence were sometimes based on love (6 percent) or ethics (6 percent), but the husband usually made the promise spontaneously in the context of a general discussion or argument about the abuse. For this reason, the promising-strategy does not have the same causal status as the other personal strategies used by the battered wives. A husband who spontaneously promised to end the abuse would be more likely to take his promise seriously than a husband who felt compelled to make such a promise. The success ratings for promises are distorted by this fact and are not comparable to the success ratings for the other personal strategies. The promising-strategy was rated as fairly successful in 5 percent of the incidents, neither successful nor unsuccessful in 63 percent of the incidents, fairly unsuccessful in 31 percent of the incidents, and very unsuccessful in 2 percent of the incidents.

Bad as this successfulness-rating is, the anecdotal material about the results of the promising-strategy in those incidents in which the wife attempted to extract a promise from her husband (instead of his promising without her urging) are more negative still. Some of the men would apologize and cry after each incident, promising never to abuse their wives again; but they usually forgot their promises when they became enraged at their wives in some future incident. Other men would apologize and make promises when sober, and then return to the abuse when inebriated. Women who were initially convinced that their husbands were sincere when making these promises eventually learned to ignore them and to realize the place of promises in the cycle of violence. Table 4–1 shows a rather consistent proportion of incidents leading to promises, with promises being most common in the worst incident and least common in the first and second incidents.

Threatening

In 23 percent of the incidents the women threatened their husbands not with violence (which would be counted as an aggressive defensive technique in this study) but with some sort of nonviolent action. This strategy consisted mainly of threatening to call the police (43 percent) and threatening to obtain a legal separation or divorce (49 percent). Nonviolent threats were the most successful of all of the self-help strategies used by wives. The women rated the strategy of threatening as very successful in 3 percent of the incidents, fairly successful in 67 percent of the incidents, neither successful nor unsuccessful in 20 percent of the incidents, and fairly unsuccessful in 11 percent of the incidents. The husbands continued their abuse in only 6 percent of the incidents, and threatened escalated abuse in an additional 7 percent of the incidents. A number of them agreed to stop the abuse but were not convincing (33 percent), and the husbands in a majority of the incidents (54 percent) apologized for the abuse and became agreeable. It is unfortunate that the women tried this strategy less frequently than other personal efforts, but it is probable that most of them did not realize the potential successfulness of the strategy until late in the series of abusive incidents that they suffered. The strategy of threatening was used in only 10 percent of the first and second battering incidents, as compared with 22 percent of the third incidents, 30 percent of the worst incidents, and 38 percent of the last incidents. Jennifer and Cynthia illustrate the use of the threatening-strategy.

> Jennifer had always been straight with Howard. When she said something, he knew she meant it. After the third violent incident, none of which involved any serious injuries, she sat Howard down and made clear that she'd leave him if he ever hit her again. She made her point vividly, saying that he would one day come home to an empty house—no wife, no children, and no forwarding address. Howard didn't think she was bluffing, so he began to tone down his rage and to avoid incidents in which he might become angry enough to hit her.

> Cynthia lived in fear of Dick for years until she saw a lawyer, who advised her to file for divorce. She still wanted to save her marriage if possible but realized that the threat of a divorce could make Dick think twice about continuing to batter her. As a respected member of the community, he had built a successful business which might be hurt by a divorce and publicity about his violence at home. An initial threat to file for divorce didn't work because Dick didn't believe her. She then instructed her lawyer to prepare the papers and showed them to Dick. He quickly agreed to refrain from further violence in return for her dropping the divorce. To keep him in line, she suspended rather than completely dropped the divorce, keeping the completed papers in her lawyer's office. Cynthia's lawyer wrote Dick letting him know that the divorce could be reactivated by no more than a phone call from her.

The women who were most successful with the strategy were those who were able to convince their husbands that the threats were serious, not frivolous. The husband had to believe that a high probability existed that the wife would follow through on the threat if he did not end his abuse. For this reason, the successful use of threatening was often combined with the involvement of a formal help-source. Some women made arrangements with an attorney for divorce proceedings to begin, so that their threat to divorce was a very immediate one. Others called the police or contacted the district attorney as the base for later successful uses of the threatening-strategy. Finally, the threatening-strategy was successful in a number of cases because it forced the husbands to agree to enter into treatment for their abusive behavior. Had they not entered treatment, it is entirely possible that the successfulness of the threatening-strategy would have been much lower in these relationships.

Hiding

The strategy of hiding consists mainly of running out of the house (70 percent of all hiding attempts), hiding in another room (20 percent), or hiding behind furniture (8 percent). Hiding was used by the women in 26 percent of the battering incidents. It was sometimes effective in ending the incidents, but it did not contribute to the permanent cessation of marital violence. In table 4–1, we see that the use of hiding peaked in the third battering incident and declined from there to the worst and the last incidents.

The use of hiding was rated as very successful in 2 percent of the incidents, fairly successful in 56 percent of the incidents, neither successful nor unsuccessful in 24 percent of the incidents, fairly unsuccessful in 15 percent of the incidents, and very unsuccessful in 4 percent of the incidents. Hiding, which also includes escape, will obviously be successful to the extent that it removes the victim from the site of the battering. This removal is not without personal cost, however. Women who spend days in living the bathrooms, attics, or cellars (years in some cases) or nights living in the woods or backyard, seriously disrupt their normal life patterns. There are two other disadvantages associated with the use of hiding. First, husbands may increase the level of abuse in response to their wives' hiding, perhaps after they have broken down doors to reach them or locked the front door and ripped their wives' clothing to keep them from leaving the house. Second, some of the women who left their houses had nowhere to go and were thus compelled to eventually return. Violent husbands who control all the resources in a marriage leave their wives with a very limited set of alternatives for escaping and hiding from the batterings.

Passive Defense

An instinctive reaction when suffering an assault is an attempt to passively defend oneself by covering the body with one's hands, arms, and feet. Despite being the most commonly used strategy (90 percent of all incidents), passive defense almost never had a positive effect on the men's behavior.

In a few cases, passive defense served to make them more angry, and they intensified the abuse.

Passive-defense techniques also have an interactional component. Covering the body with hands, arms, and feet is usually associated with crying or other indications of submission to the husband's dominance. In a few cases, the husbands were moved to end the violence by the crying, which made them realize how much they were hurting their wives. In other cases, it seemed to stimulate their sadism. The battered wives rated the technique of passive defense as fairly successful in 1 percent of the incidents, neither successful nor unsuccessful in 93 percent of the incidents, fairly unsuccessful in 5 percent of the incidents, and very unsuccessful in 1 percent of the incidents.

Aggressive Defense Techniques

The battered wives in the Milwaukee study were much less likely to use the strategy of aggressive defense than the strategy of passive defense. It was used in 29 percent of the battering incidents. The most common aggressive-defense technique was to kick, bite, or hit with a fist (53 percent of all aggressive defensive incidents). Other common aggressive-defense techniques were slapping (18 percent), hitting or trying to hit with a hard object (14 percent), and throwing something hard (5 percent). Aggressive-defense techniques proved to be dangerous in that they often made the husbands more angry and intensified the abuse (42 percent), but they also led to the termination of the violence and an apology in 26 percent of the incidents. The women gave the strategy of aggressive defense a rating of very successful in 2 percent of the incidents in which it was attempted, fairly successful in 40 percent of the incidents, neither successful nor unsuccessful in 14 percent, fairly unsuccessful in 40 percent, and very unsuccessful in 4 percent.

The use of aggressive defense increased unevenly from the first battering incident to the worst battering incident, being used in 39 percent of all of the worst incidents suffered by the women in the sample. By the last incident, it had declined to 28 percent. Aggressive-defense strategies consisted of both overt violence and threats of violence. Objects used by the women to defend themselves included furniture, kitchen utensils, telephones, and anything else at hand. The use of a knife or poison was much less common, but it had a significant effect in ending or decreasing the violence in a few of the relationships. Threats appeared to work when the husbands were convinced that the women were serious. These threats usually involved pointing out to the husband that he could not be on guard at every moment, particularly when he was sleeping, and that she would kill him at some future time when he was not expecting it if he continued his abusive behavior. Some husbands decreased or eliminated their abusive behavior because they were genuinely afraid of the threats made by their wives; other husbands were shocked by the threats and perhaps came to realize more fully the seriousness of their own behavior; and a few husbands appeared to respect their wives more for their having fought back. In these later cases, the wives achieved some status in the eyes of their husbands by engaging in behavior that was respected in what we hypothesize to be the husbands' peer subculture of violence. They thus received the same respect that would be due to a welterweight boxer who was willing to take on a heavyweight boxer and who, although losing the contest, put up a fine fight. For example, here is how Kathy freed herself from her husband's violence.

> When the violence began, Kathy had no idea what to do to protect herself. She tried avoidance, hiding, passive defense, talking, and threatening, all with no effect. Terry liked to slap her around and then force her to have sex with him on the floor. One evening after a particularly tense day, Kathy became so angry that she forgot her fear and grabbed a knife, slashing Terry's arm. She was shocked at what she had done but not any more shocked than her husband was. He immediately broke off the fight and went to the hospital for stitches. After that incident, Kathy always fought back, though never again with a deadly weapon. Fighting back didn't cause the violence to permanently come to an end. Instead, Kathy gained in self-confidence and Terry increased his respect for her. Their marriage became more of an equal partnership, which made it possible for Kathy to convince him to join her in marital counseling two years after the incident with the knife.

Avoidance

The women attempted to avoid an assault (or further assaults) in just over half of the battering incidents, mainly by keeping out of their husbands' sight or by failing to engage in an argument initiated by their husbands. In some cases, the women contrived to leave home before their husbands arrived from work when they felt there was a high probability of a battering incident.

Avoidance was used by 42 percent of the women in their first experience with marital violence. It gradually became more popular up to the worst battering incident, when 55 percent of the women were using avoidance techniques and then declined to 51 percent in the last battering incident. Like hiding, avoidance meant that these women had to surrender part of their freedom in return for a chance of decreasing the frequency or severity of their husbands' violence against them. The women rated the use of avoidance as fairly successful in 61 percent of the cases, neither successful nor unsuccessful in 36 percent of the cases, and fairly unsuccessful in 3 percent of the cases.

Relationship between Background Variables and Success of the Wife's Personal Strategies

Do various personal defensive strategies work better for some women than for others? If so, what are the personal strategies that seem to work best for each type of battered wife? Alternatively, the successfulness of the personal strategies may vary more by the characteristics of the husbands than the characteristics of the wives. Table 4–2 displays the bivariate correlations between a selection of background variables and the seven personal strategies that have been described above. It is apparent that the personal strategies were, in general, equally successful for all women regardless of their age, current occupation, mother's occupation, current income, and current marital status. Among the exceptions to this are that the promising strategy worked best for younger women and for women who remained permanently married after the termination of the violence; hiding worked best for older women and those with higher current incomes; aggressive defense worked best for women with lower current incomes; and avoidance was most successful for older women. There was also little differential successfulness among the strategies when analyzed in terms of the husband's demographic characteristics. The main exception to this generalization is that hiding worked best with husbands having higher-status occupations.

Of the four joint demographic characteristics listed in table 4–2, the only one with any appreciable influence on the success of the wife's personal strategies is the date of marriage. Women who were more recently married found lower success with the strategies of avoidance and hiding, and higher success with the strategies of promising and passive defense than did women who were married earlier. It is not clear to what extent this indicates generational changes and to what extent this is a reflection of the different ages of the women.

The previous experiences of the wife and husband with violence at the hands of their parents were only infrequently related to the success of the wife's personal strategies at correlations above ± .15, and the incidence of premarital violence was related mainly to aggressive defense and avoidance. In both cases, these strategies were more successful for women who had not experienced premarital violence than for those who had. Social embedment variables were also weakly related to the success of the wife's personal strategies.

Table 4–2
Relationships between Differentiating Variables and Success of Wife's Strategies in Last Incident

Differentiating Variables	Success of Wife's Personal Strategies						
	Talk	Promise	Threaten	Hide	Passive Defense	Aggressive Defense	Avoidance
Wife's Demographic Characteristics							
Mother's occupation	.17	.00	.08	-.12	.02	.19	-.03
Occupation	.10	-.12	.19	-.11	-.09	-.03	.12
Age	-.10	-.19	.16	.31	-.15	.02	.26
Current marital status	.16	.35	.15	.13	-.04	-.15	-.04
Current income	-.03	-.06	-.04	.31	.08	-.27	.15
Husband's Demographic Characteristics							
Parental income	.04	-.07	.05	.00	.24	-.38	-.07
Mother's occupation	-.12	.01	.03	-.07	.17	-.10	-.09
Occupation	-.14	-.07	-.11	.46	-.14	.12	.07
Education	.11	.19	.07	.10	.04	.07	.23
Armed forces	-.16	-.10	.04	.00	-.15	-.01	-.22
Saw combat	.19	.17	-.15	-.38	.11	-.24	-.22
Joint Demographic Characteristics							
Year married	.11	.19	-.17	-.29	.17	-.08	-.25
Number of children	-.01	.10	.11	.20	-.14	-.04	.11
Parental income dissimilarity	.06	.17	.13	.14	.07	-.10	.04
Occupational dissimilarity	-.11	.11	-.22	.16	.01	.15	-.15
Previous Experience With Violence							
Wife assaulted by parents	.15	-.02	.08	-.19	-.05	.10	.02
Husband assaulted by parents	.09	.04	.16	-.12	.07	.23	-.11
Premarital violence	-.13	-.05	-.06	-.03	.00	-.27	-.28
Social-Embedment Variables							
Times moved	-.08	-.18	.08	-.24	.09	.00	-.07
Wife close to relatives	-.07	.00	-.08	-.22	-.15	.20	-.20
Husband close to relatives	-.22	-.11	-.15	-.12	.02	.11	-.03
Marital Characteristics							
Reason for marriage	.20	.03	-.14	.37	-.07	.14	.22
Problem resolution—recent	-.12	-.34	.13	.01	-.18	-.05	.02
Problem resolution—earlier	.17	.30	.07	.20	-.05	.24	-.09

N=146; all correlations are Tau b

Women who married because they were pregnant were less successful at hiding and avoiding violence than women who married for more positive reasons. The promising-strategy worked better in those marriages in which the husbands were dominant than in those in which the wives were dominant during the period of the battering. However, promising worked less well in those marriages in which the husbands continued their dominance after the end of the battering. Passive defense was also less successful in these families than in those that became more equalitarian over time.

Influence of the Characteristics of Marital Violence on the Success of Wife's Use of Personal Strategies

The most immediate precursor of the wife's use of personal strategies is the violence itself. It would therefore not be surprising to find correlations between violence characteristics and the success of the personal strategies to be higher than the correlations between background variables and the success of personal strategies. This was found to be true in a few cases, but most of the correlations contained in table 4–3 are very close to zero. Three pairs of relationships are particularly interesting. The more severe the violence, the less likely women were to be successful with the strategies of talking and promising. Women whose children were assaulted were less likely than the other battered women to be successful in talking their husbands out of the abuse or in using passive-defense techniques. The longer the period of violence suffered by the women, the *more* successful they were likely to be with the strategies of threatening and avoidance.

The most important generalization that can be made about the correla-

Table 4–3
Relationships between Characteristics of Marital Violence and Success of Wife's Strategies in Last Incident

	Marital Violence Characteristics						
Success of Wife's Personal Sources	Frequency	Children Assaulted	Chemicals in Worst Incident	When Pregnant	Marital Rape	Most Severe Violence	Years c Violenc
Talk	−.21	−.32	−.13	−.05	−.16	−.41	−.08
Promise	−.20	−.18	.03	−.04	−.30	−.49	.09
Threaten	−.04	.17	.11	.25	−.05	.04	.28
Hide	.06	.06	.33	−.20	−.25	−.05	.25
Passive defense	.04	−.17	−.05	−.02	−.01	.00	−.11
Aggressive defense	−.12	.18	.11	.09	−.19	−.17	.03
Avoidance	−.18	.09	−.05	−.03	.02	−.16	.26

N=146; all correlations are Tau b

tions in table 4–3 is that the success of the talking and promising strategies depends on the quality of the relationship between husband and wife. The more serious the violence, the less likely there is to be a sufficiently healthy realtionship between husband and wife to allow these strategies to be successful in reducing marital violence.

Consistency of Successfulness among Wife's Use of Personal Strategies

The correlation matrix that is presented in table 4–4 reveals three strong relationships among the personal strategies used by the wives to combat marital violence in the final battering incident. These are between talking and promising (Tau b=.64), hiding and threatening (Tau b=−.39), and talking and passive defense (Tau b=.40). Most of the correlations are close to zero.

Correlations were also computed between the worst and the last incidents in order to test the stability of the successfulness of the individual strategies over time. These correlations proved to be extremely high. The worst-last incident correlations were: talking success, .90; promising success, .90; threatening success, .71; hiding success, .86; passive-defense success, .93; aggressive-defense success, .70; and avoidance success, .95. Although there has been only modest success in mapping the ecological distribution of the successfulness of personal strategies among different types of battered women in this chapter, it is possible to conclude that most of the women eventually found strategies that seemed to work for them and that these strategies had similar success in the worst and the last battering incidents.

Table 4–4
Intercorrelations among the Success of Wife's Strategies in Last Incident

	Talk	Promise	Threaten	Hide	Passive Defense	Aggressive Defense	Avoidance
Talk							
Promise	.64						
Threaten	.03	−.06					
Hide	−.08	−.07	−.39				
Passive defense	.40	−.02	−.16	−.04 [a]			
Aggressive defense	.21	.17	.05	[a]	[a]		
Avoidance	−.13	−.10	.10	.13	−.10	−.12	

N=146; all correlations are Tau b

[a] Less than 10 cases, or insufficient variation to compute a correlation.

5 Informal Help-Sources

Nothing is more natural than to turn to a friend or family member for help with a personal problem. The Milwaukee study examined four major sources of informal help utilized by battered wives. These are the wife's own family, in-laws, neighbors, and friends. In addition, there is the category of shelter services. Originally conceived of as a formal help-source category, shelter services were redefined as an informal help-source in response to the comments of the subjects, who usually indicated that the shelter services they had received usually came from informal help-sources rather than from a formal agency.

Family Members

Battered wives often turn to members of their own families for assistance; data were collected on 384 such incidents. Mothers were the most common family-resources, being consulted in 43 percent of these cases. Sisters (20 percent), fathers (8 percent) and brothers (11 percent) were other common sources of family help. The modal number of instances of help provided by family members was eight, and the mean was 7.2. The average length of help received was thirty-one days per incident of violence in which a wife's family member became involved.

Table 5–1 shows that at least one family member was consulted in 19 percent of the first battering incidents, increasing steadily to 43 percent of the final incidents. The most common type of help received from family members was material aid or direct service. This was extended to the beaten

Table 5–1
Proportion of Wives Using Informal Help-Sources in Five Incidents
(percentage)

Informal Help-Sources	Battering Incident				
	First	Second	Third	Worst	Last
Family	19	23	35	42	43
In-laws	12	13	16	18	16
Neighbors	10	10	12	15	17
Friends	16	23	34	50	52
Shelter services	10	12	27	28	29

N = 146

wife in 50 percent of the contacts. Other common types of help given were commanding and directing the wife about how to solve the problem (14 percent), focused talking (9 percent), direct intervention in the situation (8 percent), and listening to the battered wife (5 percent). The women were generally fairly satisfied with the help they received from family members. They rated this help as very successful in 3 percent of the incidents, fairly successful in 77 percent of the incidents, neither successful nor unsuccessful in 6 percent, and fairly unsuccessful in 14 percent. Some family members were extremely helpful, offering shelter, money, and a variety of interpersonal supports to help the wife overcome the battering. In a minority of cases, the wives were turned away by their families, sometimes being told they deserved the violence or that it was their own fault. There were even a few cases of violence occurring in front of family members who made no attempt to intervene.

In-Laws

In-laws were much less likely to be utilized as help-sources than the wife's own family members. They were approached in 12 percent of the first incidents, rising to 18 percent in the worst incidents, and then decreasing to 16 percent of the last incidents. In-laws were utilized as a source of help in a total of 167 incidents. Sisters-in-law were consulted in 20 percent of these incidents, mothers-in-law in 33 percent, and fathers-in-law in 17 percent. The modal number of sessions or instances of help associated with each incident in which an in-law became involved was three, and the mean number of sessions or instances of help was 5.4 The mean length of help following the initial contact was thirty-four days. The most common type of help received was material aid or direct service (22 percent), followed by direct intervention in the situation (19 percent), commanding or directing the wife about how to solve the problem (16 percent), and focused talking (10 percent).

Help offered by in-laws was more successful than one might expect, probably because wives did not make approaches unless they had reason to believe that in-laws might be sympathetic. The wives rated the help received from in-laws as very successful in 1 percent of the incidents, fairly successful in 51 percent of the incidents, neither successful nor unsuccessful in 13 percent, fairly unsuccessful in 32 percent, and very unsuccessful in 4 percent. Some of the in-laws were every bit as helpful as the wife's own family members. Others denied that any violence had occurred in the face of evidence to the contrary, blamed the wife for the situation, or felt impotent to do anything about it. Anecdotal evidence suggests that in-laws from violent families were less likely than other in-laws to provide support to the beaten wives. However, when in-laws chose to help the victims, they could be very effective in offering advice about dealing with their abusive husbands because of their intimate knowledge of the habits, preferences, strengths, and weaknesses of the husbands. They could therefore become formidable allies of the wife in forcing the husband to end the battering.

The following vignettes illustrate both positive and negative outcomes of battered wives' decisions to ask family members and in-laws for help.

Carrie was too embarrassed to tell her own family about being beaten by Roland, so she approached her mother-in-law, who liked her a great deal. Her mother-in-law was sympathetic, but thought there was little that could be done about the problem. She herself had been beaten by her husband since the year they were married and had never left him. She shared her priest's opinion with Carrie. He had made clear that the beatings were one of the mysteries of God's will. A good wife had to turn her cheek and to do her Christian duty, even if her husband was less than perfect.

Carrie felt better after their talk. She tried harder to please Roland, with little luck. The violence erupted regularly every few weeks during the next year. Carrie finally became so desperate to get help that she overcame her embarrassment and told her sister the entire story. Her sister and brother-in-law were both outraged when they found out how Carrie had been suffering. They invited her to bring her son and move in with them until the violence problem was settled. Then they cornered Roland and confronted him with his misbehavior, making him understand that Carrie would not move back home until he convinced them all that he would never again lay a hand on her. Roland resisted and then gave in after thinking about it for a week. When Carrie moved back in she posted her sister's number above the phone, along with the numbers of the police and a lawyer who had been recommended by the women's crisis line.

Erika's mother strongly supported her efforts to force Leonard to begin treating her with respect. His violence toward her was only one of many ways in which he abused her, communicating a lack of appreciation of her needs, rights, and uniqueness as a person. After a particularly severe assault, Erika's mother suggested that she come and stay with her for a while, which she did. Leonard was initially furious but then calmed down and eventually convinced Erika to come home. During the next three years, Erika took shelter with her mother on half-a-dozen occasions. She wanted to leave Leonard, yet her love for him was still alive, and she felt guilty over the idea of filing for a divorce. Her indecision evaporated when Leonard kicked her in the stomach after she told him that they were going to have a baby. Her mother gave her the money she needed to see an attorney and helped her to move her possessions out of the house one day while Leonard was at work. That was what finally convinced Leonard that his friends were giving him the wrong advice when they said you have to beat your wife from time to time just to let her know who is in charge. He sought and joined a therapy group for batterers, at which point Erika decided to give him another chance.

Patty's husband Arthur was a perfect gentleman while they were dating. To this day, she doesn't know why he worked so hard to deceive her until they were married. He then became unreasonable in his demands, treating her like a slave in and out of bed. Patty shared her misery with Arthur's sisters over a bottle of wine one evening while he was bowling with his friends. They told Patty that he had been violent with them on a number of occasions during their childhood. They were not at all surprised to hear that he was continuing to treat the women he cared about like dirt. Patty proposed telling the story to Arthur's parents and asking them to pressure him to cease his assaults on her. His sisters convinced her not to do this by pointing out that their mother was not well and would be terribly upset if she learned what was going on. Besides, they were terrified that Arthur would beat them up if he ever learned that they had talked with Patty about his violence. In an offhand remark, one sister mentioned that a friend of hers had received a great deal of help through a local battered-women's group, and that started Patty on the road to a violence-free life.

Neighbors

Neighbors were the least commonly used informal source of help. They became involved in 120 of the incidents, rising steadily from 10 percent of the first battering incidents to 17 percent of the last battering incidents. The modal number of sessions or instances of help was three per incident and the mean was 6.4. The mean duration of help received was fifty-seven days. Like other informal help-sources, the neighbors took a considerable personal risk in becoming involved in a marital violence situation. It was not uncommon for husbands to find out about the helping activities of the neighbors and to threaten to assault them if they persisted in their involvement with the battered wives. There were a few cases in which the husbands actually did assault neighbors who were aiding the beaten wives.

Neighbors most generally provided material aid and direct service to the battered women. This occurred in 33 percent of the incidents. Other common types of help offered were direct intervention (17 percent), directing or commanding the wife about how to solve the problem (12 percent), indicating a readiness to act on behalf of the victim (12 percent), and focused talking (9 percent). Those neighbors who offered shelter services to the wives were also at a disadvantage, because it was relatively easy for the husbands to locate their wives. Accounts of neighbors who demonstrated bystander apathy and refused to intervene were more than balanced by reports of help received, including providing transportation to the hospital, calling the police at a prearranged signal, and providing a ready sanctuary from the abuse. Help received from neighbors was rated by the battered wives as very successful in 4 percent of the incidents, fairly successful in 71 percent, neither successful nor unsuccessful in 5 percent, fairly unsuccessful in 15 percent, and very unsuccessful in 4 percent.

Some neighbors courageously confront the batterer with his behavior, and others indicate willingness to physically intervene with the batterer on behalf of his wife. Monica and George did precisely that when they learned of the living hell that Lucy was going through.

> Lucy and Mel moved into the house next door to Monica and George in 1978. Shortly thereafter, they heard a knock on the door late one evening. It was Lucy, whose face showed why she was there. At first, they thought that Lucy had been assaulted by a burglar, and Monica wanted to call the police. Lucy said no, and explained how Mel had beaten her up for having talked to another man while they were in a bar earlier in the evening. She came over for help after Mel passed out on the couch.

> The next week, Mel was sitting on the patio when George came up to share a beer with him. After some small talk about sports, George let Mel know what he thought of men who beat their wives. Mel suspected that Lucy had talked to George, or at least to Monica, but George didn't say anything personal and Mel didn't dare bring anything up that would reveal his assaultiveness toward Lucy. After George left, Mel hurried in the house and lunged at Lucy in a fury, accusing her of having talked behind his back. Lucy ran out the front door and into Monica and George's house. Monica had the presence of mind to lock the door behind Lucy, and Mel made quite a scene on the porch trying to get in. He was still fuming when the police arrived. George and Monica helped Lucy to be assertive with the less-than-friendly police officer, who tried to discourage her from filing assault charges. Without their help, Lucy would probably never have enlisted the aid of the criminal-justice system to end the violence in her life.

Friends

Friends were the second most common informal help-source consulted at the time of the first battering, and they became steadily more important in the effort to end the battering from incident to incident, reaching 52 percent by the last incident. The modal number of sessions or other instances of help received from friends in the 380 incidents in which they participated was eight, and the mean was 7.9. The mean duration of help received was eighty-four days per incident. Material aid or direct service was the primary nature of the help received in 31 percent of the incidents. Other common types of help received were directing or commanding about problem solving (28 percent), focused talking (19 percent), and direct intervention on behalf of the beaten women (8 percent).

The victims of the abuse gave very high successfulness ratings to the help received from their friends. Three precent of their interventions were rated as very successful, 81 percent as fairly successful, 7 percent as neither successful nor unsuccessful, 9 percent as fairly unsuccessful, and 1 percent as very unsuccessful. The most important theme expressed by the battered women about the help received from friends was that the strong interpersonal support enabled them to strengthen their self-confidence, which was often a prerequisite for any other actions taken against their husbands. Asking for help in a battering situation is one of the supreme tests of a friend, and those who failed the test ran the risk of having their friendships with the victims reevaluated.

Rhoda was a military wife, spending much of her time on army bases overseas. Byron was a tense, hard-driving career soldier. He put so much of himself into his job that he had little left over for her needs. Most of his recreational pursuits occurred with his military buddies while Rhoda sat home alone. When he would have a particularly threatening day at the office, he would become so upset that he would slam doors and throw furniture around the house. During those periods of great tension, Rhoda had to watch every word she said. Her slightest disagreement or criticism, which showed insufficient sympathy and support—even an attempt to change the conversation to a more pleasant subject—swiftly brought her a slap or a kick from Byron.

When Byron lost out on an important promotion, he beat her up so badly that she could hardly walk. There was no place on the base to which she could go for help without great danger that Byron would find out, and he had said that he'd kill her if she revealed their secret—he thought it would ruin his career. Rhoda was beside herself and spilled out the details of her life with Byron to her good friend Donna. Over the next few weeks, they got together almost daily to talk about what Rhoda should do. Seeing herself and the violence through Donna's eyes, Rhoda came to realize that there was no reason for her to allow Byron to mistreat her so badly. He had a problem, and instead of seeking help to deal with it, he was unfairly taking things out on her.

As Rhoda's self-confidence grew, she realized that it would take a dramatic gesture on her part to reestablish a worthwhile relationship with Bryon. She also began to seriously consider the possibility of a divorce for the first time. Donna loaned her the money for a plane ticket, and one day after Byron went to work, Rhoda slipped out and flew to visit with her sister. Byron was frantic when he read her note, but she refused to accept a call from him for a week. When she finally did talk to him, she told him that he would never be able to batter her again. Either he agreed to change his ways or she wasn't ever coming back. He readily agreed—too readily for Rhoda to believe him. Now that Donna helped her to feel better about herself, she didn't intend to go back to a life of violence. She demanded that Byron see the psychiatrist on the post to work out his tensions and frustrations. Byron initially balked at what he thought an embarrassment and then agreed when Rhoda refused to give in. For good measure, she waited until he'd seen the psychiatrist twice before she flew home

Shelter Services

Many of the women in the sample reported spousal abuse that occurred some years ago, before the first battered-women's shelter was opened in the United States. Even today, the number of shelters in southeastern Wisconsin is grossly inadequate to meet the need for shelter services that exists among these victims of spousal assault. It is fortunate that friends, neighbors, and family members are often willing to step forward and offer shelter services to the beaten wives, sometimes for periods of many months.

There were 204 incidents which led to the use of shelter by the battered women. Only 10 percent of the victims utilized shelter services after the first battering incident, but this rose steadily to 29 percent of the women in the last battering incident. In a quarter of these incidents, the length of stay was one day or less. The mean length of stay was twenty-seven days, but that was inflated by the small number of incidents in which the women received shelter services for six or more months. The modal length of shelter services received was fifteen days. In 139 of the incidents, the children in the family accompanied the wife into the shelter.

The most common source of shelter services was the wife's relatives (56 percent), followed by friends and neighbors (23 percent), and women's resource centers (5 percent). Naturally, the primary category of help given through shelter services was material aid and direct service, but their unconditional availability was the most important aspect of the help received in fifteen of the instances in which these services were used. The shelter services received were rated as very successful by 12 percent of the battered women, fairly successful by 84 percent, neither successful nor unsuccessful by 3 percent, and fairly unsuccessful by 1 percent.

Influence of Background Variables and Marital Violence
Characteristics on the Success of Informal Help-Sources

Table 5–2 presents information about the relationships between demographic characteristics, previous experiences with violence, social embedment, and marital characteristics, on the one hand, and the success of the five informal help-sources, on the other hand. A third of the 120 relationships summarized in this table reach ± .15. The use of neighbors was more likely to be successful for older wives and for those having husbands with relatively high-status occupations and relatively low educational levels. The success of services received from family members was more often high if the husband had been assaulted by his parents and if the wife was close to her own relatives. Help received from in-laws was generally more successful in

Table 5-2
Relationships between Differentiating Variables and Successfulness of Informal Help-Sources in Last Incident

Differentiating Variables	Success of Informal Help-Sources				
	Family	In-Laws	Neighbors	Friends	Shelter Services
Wife's demographic characteristics					
Mother's occupation	-.10	.02	.16	.17	-.21
Occupation	-.06	.28	.12	.01	-.02
Age	-.06	-.10	.33	.08	.10
Current marital status	.05	.29	.26	-.05	.01
Current income	-.11	.00	.06	.03	-.01
Husband's demographic charcteristics					
Parental income	.08	a	a	.02	a
Mother's occupation	.19	.16	-.06	.17	.14
Occupation	-.16	-.09	.43	.11	-.10
Education	-.16	-.07	-.39	-.06	-.12
Armed forces	-.09	.07	.27	-.22	.20
Saw combat	-.09	-.18	-.19	-.22	-.17
Joint demographic characteristics					
Year married	-.01	.02	-.30	-.10	-.05
Number of children	.10	.08	.26	-.06	-.12
Parental income dissimilarity	-.12	.33	-.28	-.20	-.06
Occupational dissimilarity	-.07	-.26	.18	.02	-.02
Previous experience with violence					
Wife assaulted by parents	-.05	-.35	-.11	.05	-.25
Husband assaulted by parents	.30	-.24	.01	.16	.05
Premarital violence	-.15	.00	-.18	.13	.21
Social-embedment variables					
Times moved	.01	.04	.22	.06	.10
Wife close to relatives	.22	.19	-.23	-.07	-.16
Husband close to relatives	-.17	-.29	.27	.15	-.08
Marital characteristics					
Reason for marriage	-.10	.01	-.05	.00	-.18
Problem resolution-recent	.06	-.37	-.07	-.09	-.24
Problem resolution-earlier	-.06	-.41	a	-.06	-.04

N = 146; all correlations are Tau b

[a] Less than 10 cases, or insufficient variation to compute a correlation.

those families in which the wife had a higher-status background than the husband. Help from in-laws was less successful in those families in which the wife had been assaulted by her parents and in which husbands no longer continued to dominate the marital decision-making process after the cessation of violence. The success of shelter services was greatest for wives who had not been beaten by their parents and whose husbands did not dominate the decision-making processes after the battering ended. Relationships involving the successfulness of help received from friends and any of the background variables in table 5.2 are generally weaker than relationships with other informal help-sources.

Table 5–3 continues in the same vein, with most correlations close to zero. Two of the strongest relationships indicate that the success of help received from family members is greater in those battering relationships characterized by high frequency of violence and low use of alcohol and psychoactive drugs in the worst incident. The absense of a consistent pattern of statistically significant relationships suggests that the successfulness of informal help-sources is based on factors other than the background characteristics of the participants, the characteristics of the marital dyad, and the dimensions of the marital violence. It may be that the content of the help received from informal sources is of primary importance in its successfulness, or there may be unmeasured characteristics of the help-giver or of the helping process that could enable us to understand the observed variations in the successfulness of informal help-sources.

Correlations among the Successfulness Ratings of Informal Help-Sources

Table 5–4 presents the correlation matrix for the wife's use of informal help-sources to combat the marital violence in the last battering incident. Four of the cells in the matrix do not have enough cases for the computation of a correlation coefficient due to a shortage of subjects who use both of the two intersecting informal help-sources in relation to the same incident. The two strongest relationships found in table 5–4 are between the use of shelter services and help received from neighbors (Tau b = .49) and friends (Tau b= .43).

The correlations for the success of informal help-sources in the worst and the last incidents are somewhat lower than they are for the wife's own strategies (see chapter 4). The correlations are .60 for family members, .76 for friends, and .60 for shelter services. There were not enough cases in which in-laws and neighbors were utilized as sources of help in both the worst and last incidents to permit the computation of a correlation coefficient.

Table 5-3

Relationships between Characteristics of Marital Violence and Success of Informal Help-Sources in Last Incident

Success of Informal Help-Sources	Marital Violence Characteristics						
	Frequency	Children Assaulted	Chemicals in Worst Incident	When Pregnant	Marital Rape	Most Severe Violence	Years of Violence
Family	.25	.11	-.21	.14	.12	.11	-.06
In-laws	-.05	-.18	.15	.16	.00	.06	.15
Neighbors	.09	.11	.12	.00	-.14	.13	.15
Friends	.13	.00	-.18	.20	.02	-.03	.13
Shelter services	-.01	-.14	.02	.09	.03	-.11	.01

N = 146; All correlations are Tau b

Table 5–4

Intercorrelations among the Success of Informal Help-Sources in Last Incident

	Family	In-Laws	Neighbors	Friends	Shelter Services
Family					
In-laws	.31				
Neighbors	a	a			
Friends	.26	a	.27		
Shelter services	.02	a	.49	.43	

N = 146; all correlations are Tau b

[a] Less than 10 cases, or insufficient variation to compute a correlation.

Formal Help-Sources

Formal help-sources are officially sanctioned by the community. They have a stable organizational structure, specified resources and services, and either legal or moral power to persuade individuals to take them seriously. Four formal help-sources were examined in the study, plus a fifth that might best be described as semi-formal: police, social-service agencies, lawyers and district attorneys, clergy, and women's groups. Women's groups are viewed as semi-formal rather than formal because they are less established and organizationally structured, and have extremely limited moral power (and no legal power at all) to compel individuals to give up their assaultive behavior.

The Police

The police become involved in spousal assaults in a very different way than other formal help-sources. They are not contacted between assaults but are called during the assaults. Police do not provide a specific, highly technical service; they provide generalized support-services for which they are often inadequately trained. The battered wives requested help from the police in connection with 276 incidents. In all but 14 percent of these incidents, the help they received consisted of a single contact. The police were called in 9 percent of the first battering incidents. This rose steeply to 38 percent of the worst incidents, and then declined to 34 percent in the last incidents (see table 6–1).

Nine out of every ten police involvements occurred at the request of the wives, with most of the remaining involvements coming in response to calls

Table 6–1
Proportion of Wives Using Formal Help-Sources in Five Incidents
(percentage)

Formal Help-Sources	Battering Incident				
	First	Second	Third	Worst	Last
Police	9	16	25	38	34
Social-service agencies	7	10	16	30	43
Lawyers and district attorneys	6	5	12	35	49
Clergy	8	10	14	16	15
Women's groups	1	3	8	21	36

N = 146

by neighbors and friends. Once called, the police usually arrived within fifteen minutes, and they took more than twenty minutes to arrive in only one out of every ten cases. There were very few incidents in which the police refused to come or said they would come and then did not appear. The primary reason women called the police was fear for their lives; this occurred in 59 percent of the incidents in which the police were called. An additional 32 percent called because they had experienced enough abuse and wanted to impress upon their husbands the seriousness of their determination to end the violence. As one might expect, the most common service delivered by the police was to intervene directly to diminish the source of stress, and occurred in 32 percent of the incidents. Other common services received were to provide material aid and direct services (15 percent), focused talking (6 percent), and listening (5 percent).

The range of services delivered by the police is amazing in view of their relatively narrow law-enforcement mission. In addition to being asked to end the battering in some fashion, often by arresting the husband, some of the police officers who arrived on the scene were also asked to take the wife to the hospital or to the shelter of a friend or an agency, to help the wife move her belongings out of the house, to stand by in case the absent husband returned home, to provide the wife with legal advice, and to counsel the husband about the seriousness of his assaultive behavior. The police actually arrested the husband in 15 percent of the incidents, but they refused to make an arrest in 31 percent of the incidents, saying that there was no case against the batterer. In 46 percent of the incidents, the police asked the couple to reconcile their differences. There were a few cases in which the police laughed or joked with the husband, told the wife that she deserved the beatings because she did not adequately perform her wifely duties, or flirted on duty. The range of police services to battered women is depicted in the following vignettes.

Sarah called the police during more than a dozen battering incidents, mostly when Tim included the children in his violence toward her. Although the police removed Tim from the house so he could cool off on several occasions, they never carried out her request to arrest him. Tim soon realized that the police would not do anything to him, and so their repeated visits had no effect on his continued violence.

Jocelyn was so badly beaten that she went to a woman's house nearby to avoid further abuse. After discussing the situation with her neighbor, she decided to press charges and called the police. An officer came quickly and seeing her injuries, suggested that she get herself to the hospital. Other than that, he refused to become involved and ignored the battered wife. He instead struck up a conversation with the neighbor and asked her out on a date.

Penny was too afraid of Alex to call the police until the beatings were over and he was out of the house. The police felt that she should call while the beatings were in progress and told her to either learn to live with the beatings or to move out of the house. After the worst incident, one officer embarrassed Penny by staring at her ripped blouse, and his partner offered to take her to the hospital if she would find her own way home afterwards. They both said that they could not protect her from future abuse and left her feeling hopeless.

June isn't sure how often she called the police over the years but thinks it was probably more than fifty times. Most officers were helpful when they took her husband Ernie outside to cool off or made other minor attempts to improve the situation. Others were insulting, one laughing with the husband about her and another telling her that she was too old to get another man. Once she had filed for a divorce, the police became much more attentive to her needs and made clear to Ernie that they intended to protect her from further abuse. When Ernie raped her while they were legally separated, the police arrested him at her request, and they supported her in her decision to press charges.

Mary's husband Rob was so enraged that he hit her in front of a police officer, but the officer ignored the assault. Instead of arresting Rob, the officer blamed her for the beatings because she wasn't a neat housekeeper. On a later occasion, two officers were more sympathetic to her plight. Remembering her previous experience, she became afraid of what Rob would do to her after the officers left the scene and so made excuses to the officers for his violent behavior instead of asking them to arrest him.

Some of the wives relied heavily on police aid, calling them fifty times or more over a period of years. Although the response of the officers on the scene was occasionally outrageous and usually ineffective, there were a great many occasions in which they rendered exemplary service, going far beyond the call of duty in many incidents. For this reason, it is fair to say that calling the police is a game of Russian roulette, in which the quality of service received by the battered wife varies according to the characteristics of the officers who respond. Overall, the battered wives rated the police as very successful in 1 percent of the incidents, fairly successful in 33 percent, neither successful nor unsuccessful in 33 percent, fairly unsuccessful in 30 percent, and very unsuccessful in 3 percent.

Social-Service Agencies

In 283 incidents the battered wives sought help from social-service agencies. The modal number of sessions was 8 and the mean was 15.4. The mean length of service was 6.7 months per incident, which was inflated by the fact that the length of treatment in one out of every five incidents was 16 months or more. Social-service agencies became involved in 7 percent of the first battering incidents, rising slowly at first, and then more steeply to 30 percent of the worst battering incidents and 43 percent of the last battering incidents.

The battered women usually became involved with private family-counseling agencies (68 percent) or county agencies (19 percent). There was a scattering of agency involvement for drug and alcohol treatment rather than family counseling, and there were a few involvements with religious social-service agencies.

The most common service received by the battered women from these agencies was focused talking, which occurred in 32 percent of the incidents. Other common services received were commanding and directing about problem solving (31 percent), material aid and direct service (9 percent) and suggestions about problem solving (4 percent). The husbands became aware of their wives' involvement with social-service agencies in four out of every five cases, and in nearly half of these cases they participated in counseling themselves. If the couples participated in counseling together, it was likely to be helpful in enabling them to sort out the problems of their marriage. If the wife participated alone, she was likely to gain insight into her husband's behavior and to strengthen the self-confidence required to take further action to end the abuse. Overall, the battered wives had more positive experiences with social-service agencies than with the police, but there were a number of negative experiences. In these cases counselors supported the husbands against their wives, refused to deal with the battering as an important problem in the marriage, or further damaged the wives' self-images while building up their own egos. The women rated the help received from social-service agencies as very successful in 2 percent of the cases, fairly successful in 57 percent, neither successful nor unsuccessful in 22 percent, fairly unsuccessful in 17 percent, and very unsuccessful in 2 percent. The case of Audrey and Charles is typical of the social-service agency interventions in the Milwaukee sample.

Audrey and Charles went to a marital counseling program for six sessions. During this time, Charles did not deny his violence. He played it down and claimed that it was a natural part of marriage. His father hit his mother often, and Charles felt they had a good marriage. Since he consistently claimed that there was no problem in the marriage, there was no progress made in the counseling sessions. Depressed over the whole situation, Audrey also dropped out of counseling. She began to wonder whether she still had a marital relationship worth continuing.

The battering continued from time to time over the following eight months, at the end of which Audrey went to see a counselor at the nearby mental-health center. Charles didn't object since he thought she was the only one with a problem. Audrey began talking about the batterings as if they were the only problem in the marriage, but the counselor helped her to realize that it had many serious problems. As the sessions continued over the following months, Audrey stopped thinking of herself as being at fault in the batterings or as basically being a bad wife. She now defined herself as a worthwhile human being who tried hard to make a go of her marriage and who deserved a fair shake from her husband.

Having made up her mind to be a victim no longer, she made arrangements to move in with her brother's family and warned Charles that the next time he beat her would be the last. He brushed off her warning, and a violent argument occurred the following weekend. Audrey was badly beaten, but for the first time she was more determined than angry or fearful. She left Charles the next day. Audrey stayed with her brother and sister-in-law for six weeks, resisting apologies and threats alike. Only when Charles openly admitted that he had a problem about allowing her to be an equal partner in the marriage and that the violence was wrong did Audrey agree to give him one more chance. Under pressure, Charles started seeing Audrey's counselor in weekly sessions separate from her own.

Lawyers and District Attorneys

Lawyers and district attorneys were consulted slightly less frequently than were social-service agencies. The modal number of visits to a lawyer or district attorney in the 252 incidents in which this occurred was 8, and the mean was 8.1. The mean length of contact was 3.4 months. The direct involvement of the legal system was extremely limited in the first several battering incidents, but it rose sharply to 35 percent in the worst incident and 49 percent in the last incident. Like the police and most other formal help-sources, the legal profession is dominated by men. Less than one in every five of the lawyers consulted by the battered wives was a woman. The primary service received from the legal profession was material aid or direct service, in the form of legal action or movement toward legal action against the husbands. This occurred in 74 percent of the cases, and the only other type of help received in more than a handful of cases was focused talking, which occurred in 11 percent of the incidents.

The legal actions requested by the wives were mainly divorces (176 cases) or assault charges (44 cases), with a few requests for restraining orders (9 cases) and separations (6 cases). These legal actions were eventually carried out in four out of every ten incidents. Lawyers differ from the police in that they take an advocacy position in support of their clients. The role of the police officer is like that of judge, in which he or she must decide on a balanced course of action in a given case rather than automatically act on behalf of the apparent victim. District attorneys are closer to the police than to lawyers on the scale of advocacy on behalf of the victims. However, there were some cases in which the women who sought aid from district attorneys were urged to drop charges or had to be satisfied with an informal warning to the husbands. The negative experiences that the battered wives had with the legal profession included unwillingness to provide help on a weekend, attempted seductions, complete lack of concern for the wife's needs and preferences, and unwillingess to put any effort into the case unless there was a prospect of good publicity and a spectacular trial. The women rated services delivered by legal professionals as very successful in 9 percent of the cases, fairly successful in 50 percent, neither successful nor unsuccessful in 21 percent, fairly unsuccessful in 19 percent, and very unsuccessful in less than 1 percent.

The experiences of Susan, Ann, and Francine are examples of what happened when the battered wives consulted lawyers.

Susan located a militantly feminist attorney through a local women's group, and with her help, collected evidence and filed assault charges. Her husband was found guilty and placed on probation. Susan later tried to file for a divorce, but the attorney seemed strangely uninterested in helping when there was no potential for a spectacular court case. As a result, Susan gave up on a divorce and became involved in a women's support group.

Ann saw three different lawyers at different times. One made sexual advances toward her, and this shocked her so much that she did not seek further legal help for several years. The second lawyer gave accurate legal advice but advised her to continue in the marriage as long as possible. When Ann saw the third lawyer, she had become frantic to get away from her husband. This attorney found her accommodations in a safe place and did all the necessary paper work to obtain a legal separation.

Francine had already spent a year in a women's support group when she consulted a lawyer to find out whether Murray, her husband, was telling the truth when he said he'd take their children away from her if she ever left him. The lawyer seemed to have little sympathy for her plight, so she accused him of being cold and unfeeling. He apologized and became more understanding. He assured her that Murray could not take the children away from her, and Francine used this information to confront Murray and to convince him to join a therapy group for batterers.

The following vignettes illustrate what happened when the women sought help from a district attorney.

Elizabeth went to the district attorney (D.A.) after Hans broke several of her ribs, and the D.A. talked her into dropping the case. She tried again a year later, this time with a particularly bad set of bruises on her face and body. The D.A. was more sympathetic this time, and she was very pleased with the way she was treated. Hans became so angered when she recounted his beatings of her in court that he threatened her in front of the judge. As a result, he served three months in the county jail.

Stephanie said she wanted to file charges for marital rape, to which the district attorney answered that she had no evidence. However, he agreed to prosecute for assault, and her husband was placed on probation by the judge.

Nannette was referred to the county victim-witness project by her lawyer. They provided her with transportation, child care, and plenty of good advice, in addition to helping her to work with the district attorney's office in filing charges. With their assistance, she was able to follow through on the case in the face of harassment from her husband. Despite a finding of not guilty in court, Nannette was satisfied that her husband now knew that the legal establishment was willing to take an interest in her case.

Trudy tried to file a complaint with the district attorney, but he responded by showing her pictures of horribly battered wives. The D.A. said that he could not win a case unless she was as badly beaten as they were. Trudy persisted for a time, and then allowed herself to be talked out of filing charges. The only thing the D.A. did for her was to send her husband a form letter.

Battered Women and the Law

There are few institutions in the United States that are more completely dominated by men and by male values than the law. The proportion of police officers, lawyers, district attorneys, and judges who are women is extremely small. Even when women manage to work their way into the system, they are usually excluded from positions of influence and leadership. Only recently was the first woman in history appointed to the Supreme Court.

Many of the men in these professions share a masculine culture that emphasizes sports, alcohol, violence, toughness, and a set of beliefs about the inferiority of women. They believe that women tend to be hysterical, to confuse facts with emotions, to be controlled by their hormones, and to need a strong man to keep them in line because they are weak-minded. These slurs on womanhood are shared in men's bathrooms, bars, men's clubs, fraternities, on the job, at sporting events, and in any other setting from which women are largely excluded.

Favors, information, and social contacts in the legal system are not randomly distributed. They are linked to the old-boy-network. This is a network of men who believe in the values of the masculine culture and who congregate in places where women are infrequently present. Women who wish to become successful lawyers may be held back because they lack the information and favors that are available only to men who are part of the old-boy-network.

When battered women contact the police, a lawyer, or the district attorney's office, they come face-to-face with a masculine culture and the old-boy-network. Over and over, the Milwaukee women were ignored, dismissed as hysterical, disbelieved, and talked out of what they had already decided to do to defend themselves against further beatings. At the same time, their husbands sometimes exchanged friendly talk with police officers and legal officials. One might think that the husbands had been victimized by crazy women instead of their having viciously and repeatedly assaulted their wives.

Not all police officers and lawyers subscribe to the masculine culture, with its demeaning view of women. Unfortunately, the men who are more independent tend to be excluded from powerful positions and are sometimes so discouraged that they resign. In short, by refusing to be sexist, they leave themselves open for the same mistreatment that women often get. Battered women who happen to contact lawyers and police officers who are not sexist may receive more sympathetic treatment, but sexism in the system limits the effectiveness of the help they receive in the long run.

The Clergy

The clergy were as likely as any other formal help-source to be consulted after the first battering incident, but they rapidly slipped behind and were the least consulted formal help-source in the worst and last incidents. They were used as a help-source in only 15 percent of the final battering incidents. The modal number of sessions in the 132 cases in which the clergy became involved was 3, and the mean was 10.7. The mean length of service was 3.9 months, and 13 percent of the women received services for at least 18 months in connection with a battering incident. Focused talking was the most common service received from the clergy (28 percent), followed by commanding and directing about problem solving (24 percent), and material aid or direct service (11 percent).

The battered women rated services received from the clergy as very successful in 2 percent of the cases, fairly successful in 53 percent, neither successful nor unsuccessful in 22 percent, fairly unsuccessful in 22 percent, and very unsuccessful in 2 percent of the cases. The anecdotal evidence provided by the women suggests that the clergy were the most conservative advice-givers of all the formal help-sources. It was common for the clergy to do their best to keep the couple together regardless of the consequences for the wife's welfare. Although many of the clergy gave exemplary service under difficult conditions, some risking assaults by the husbands, there were also a number of incidents in which the clergy blamed the wives for their own victimization or otherwise responded unsympathetically or unprofessionally to the victims' requests for assistance. Both successful and unsuccessful clerical interventions are described in vignettes about Irene, Judith, Constance, and Libby.

> Irene went to a priest and told him the full story of the beatings she had suffered. He said that he would pray for her, but that it was her Christian duty to stay with her abusive husband forever. He advised her to make the best of a bad situation and said that an annulment or a divorce was out of the question. She did what she could to please her husband for another year but then sought the aid of a social-service agency. Because he also assaulted the children on occasion, she was able to have him removed from the home.

Judith, in desperation, finally broached the subject of her husband's abusiveness with her minister. He at first refused to believe her. Then, when she showed him some convincing bruises and scars, he accepted her story. His attack on her continued, however, as he now accused her of provoking the abuse by being bitchy and keeping a messy house. Judith was so shattered by this experience that she switched to another church.

Constance was a devoutly religious woman. When her husband of three years first assaulted her, she locked herself in the bedroom and called her minister. He came immediately and argued strenuously with her spouse, who was still enraged. When her husband punched the minister in the face after he refused to leave, she called the police and had him arrested. Despite this terrifying experience, the minister counseled the couple over a period of months and held no grudge against the batterer. She agreed to drop the complaint she had filed after her husband promised never again to assault her.

Libby talked over her marriage with a priest, who suggested that she and her husband come in together for counseling. She was able to convince her husband to accompany her to the next session, but when she mentioned his violence toward her, he flew into a rage and denied everything. When they got home, he assaulted her again to put her in her place. As soon as he left the house, she called the priest, who immediately picked her up and took her to a Catholic retreat. He then sought out her husband and shamed him into entering counseling for both his violence and his drinking problem.

Women's Groups

The final formal help-source utilized by the battered wives is women's groups. These groups need not be feminist in orientation, although a number of them are. Involvement with a women's group occurred in connection with 197 of the battering incidents. The modal number of sessions per incident was 8, and the mean was 19.0. The mean length of service was 8.5 months, and the battered wives received more than 18 months of services in 28 percent of the incidents. Twenty-nine percent of the women's groups were operated by feminist organizations devoted to the welfare of battered women, 29 were sponsored by Alanon or Alcoholics Anonymous, and the other groups were sponsored primarily by social-service agencies (29 percent) or religious organizations (11 percent). Because of the incomplete institutionalization of women's groups as formal help-sources, they often are found under a wide variety of auspices, and they usually lack the funds necessary to purchase their own facilities.

In table 6–1, we see that women's groups were rarely consulted after the early battering incidents, with their involvement rising to 21 percent of the worst incidents and 36 percent of the last incidents. This reflects the increase in the availability of women's groups in recent years at least as much as changes in the help-seeking activities of the battered wives between the first and the last incidents. The service offered most frequently to battered wives by the women's groups was modeling. In this type of help, women who had successfully triumphed over the problem of spousal abuse explained to currently battered women how they came to be victors instead of victims. This occurred in a relatively equalitarian setting, usually involving group activites rather than one-on-one activities between a therapist and a client. Other common services provided by the women's groups were material aid and direct service (20 percent), focused talking (8 percent), and suggestions about problem solving (4 percent).

The wives described their experiences with women's groups in glowing terms. The modeling technique appears to be extremely successful in enabling them to increase their reality-testing ability and to build up their self-images. The most negative aspect of the battered wives' involvement in women's groups was the threat that this involvement posed for many of their husbands. In some cases, this probably resulted in a temporary increase in the violence until the wife gained enough strength to compel the husband to desist. Take the case of Iris as an example.

Iris was not beaten until the third year of her marriage to Craig, when he began to drink heavily. Although Craig also battered her when sober, the general collapse of his hopes for a successful career seemed to have set off both his violence toward her and a severe drinking problem. When Iris confided in her friend, she learned that Alcoholics Anonymous could be very helpful to Craig. He refused to even try one meeting when she brought up the subject, so she had to be content with joining Alanon to find out more about alcoholism and to try to work out a method of dealing with Craig's rapid deterioration. In an Alanon group with other wives who had similar problems with their husbands, Iris received a great deal of support and also gained insight into what had been happening to Craig.

One of the women in Alanon simultaneously belonged to a women's group sponsored by a nearby battered-women's shelter. As they became close friends, she convinced Iris to come to the group with her. At this point, Iris decided to tell Craig what she was doing. He was threatened by the idea that she was "running around with a bunch of feminists who were out to destroy the family," and ordered her to immediately resign from the group. She refused, receiving a series of harsh punches and kicks as a result. They fought over her participating in the group again and again in the next four weeks, but Craig eventually gave up, perhaps because Iris had convinced him that the group was neither radically feminist nor against her remaining with Craig if that was what she decided to do. Several group members had left their husbands, two were undecided, and the others definitely wanted to salvage their marriages if they could obtain their husbands' cooperation.

Through her participation in the group, Iris realized that she had the power to break the cycle of Craig's violence by refusing to become involved in senseless arguments and by staying away from Craig when he was drinking heavily. After one particularly bad beating, a member of the group invited her to stay at her apartment while she recovered. They discussed filing charges for assault, but Iris felt this would only make the situation worse. Following a lengthy session with the women's group, she decided to take action to end both Craig's violence and his excessive drinking. She gave him an ultimatum, either he would enter counseling within thirty days or she would file for a divorce. Thanks to her experiences in the women's group, Iris knew that she had the strength to live alone if Craig refused to enter treatment.

Relationships between Background Variables, Marital Violence Characteristics, and the Success of Formal Help-Sources

A glance at table 6–2 convinces us that the success of formal help-sources is as little differentiated by the background characteristics and marital violence dimensions of the couples as were the informal help-source success ratings. Like these evaluations, the formal ratings are limited to successfulness in the last battering incident, so the number of cases in each cell is usually much less than the sample size. The stronger relationships between demographic characteristics and formal help-sources show that women who continued to stay married to their husbands after the cessation of the violence received more successful services from the police, lawyers and district attorneys, and the clergy than did the other battered wives; and the success of services received from the clergy was directly related to the husband's educational level. Other relationships involving the other background variables and the success of formal help-sources suggest that (1) families in which the husband was assaulted by his parents are less likely to have successful experiences with social-service agencies; (2) families in which there was premarital violence or in which the husband was close to his relatives were less likely to receive successful services from the clergy; and (3) families that became more equalitarian after the cessation of the violence were less likely to have had successful experiences with lawyers and district attorneys.

Few of the relationships portrayed in table 6–3 reach ± .15. Among the connections between marital violence characteristics and the successful use of formal help-sources in the last battering incident are that (1) the successfulness of police services is inversely related to assaults on children; (2) the success of services received from social-service agencies is directly related to the prevalence of marital rape; and (3) the success of services received from the clergy is inversely related to the frequency of violence and to violence when pregnant. As was the case with the success of informal help-sources received in the last battering incident, it appears that the variation in the success of help received is not explained by either background variables or

Table 6–2
Relationships between Differentiating Variables and Successfulness of Formal Help-Sources in Last Incident

Differentiating Variables	Formal Help-Sources				
	Police	Social Agencies	Lawyers D.A.s	Clergy	Women's Groups
Wife's demographic characteristics					
Mother's occupation	.03	-.09	-.05	.17	-.10
Occupation	.09	.00	.16	-.17	.06
Age	.14	.15	.02	.13	-.03
Current marital status	.22	-.09	.25	.37	.12
Current income	.20	.08	-.09	-.32	-.03
Husband's demographic characteristics					
Parental income	.26	.06	-.14	a	-.20
Mother's occupation	-.04	.10	-.04	.31	-.03
Occupation	.19	-.17	.01	.22	.04
Education	.02	-.07	.16	.43	-.15
Armed forces	-.03	.13	-.01	-.31	-.12
Saw combat	-.09	.20	-.21	-.03	-.04
Joint demographic characteristics					
Year married	-.08	-.16	-.05	.02	-.01
Number of children	-.07	.17	-.09	-.01	.03
Parental income dissimilarity	-.05	-.07	.12	.35	.01
Occupational dissimilarity	.09	.03	-.12	-.04	.06
Previous experience with violence					
Wife assaulted by parents	.11	-.07	.06	.18	.03
Husband assaulted by parents	-.17	-.29	-.08	.02	.09
Premarital violence	.03	.06	.03	-.88	.04
Social-embedment variables					
Times moved	-.02	-.13	.08	-.04	-.01
Wife close to relatives	-.02	-.01	.19	-.02	-.10
Husband close to relatives	-.22	-.02	.10	-.41	-.14
Marital characteristics					
Reason for marriage	.13	.01	.04	.01	.12
Problem resolution—recent	-.10	.13	-.23	.26	.10
Problem resolution—earlier	-.08	-.10	.07	-.14	-.19

N=146; all correlations are Tau b

Table 6–3
Relationships between Characteristics of Marital Violence and Success of Formal Help-Sources in Last Incident

Success of Formal Help-Sources	Marital Violence Characteristics						
	Frequency	Children Assaulted	Chemicals in Worst Incident	When Pregnant	Marital Rape	Most Severe Violence	Years of Violence
Police	-.11	-.23	-.09	-.15	-.03	.02	.03
Social-service agencies	.05	-.11	.14	.02	.28	-.02	.18
Lawyers and district attorneys	.01	-.10	-.02	.02	-.14	-.15	-.12
Clergy	-.47	-.03	.02	-.43	-.27	.14	-.12
Women's groups	.00	-.04	.00	-.04	-.01	.06	.02

N = 146; all correlations are Tau b

marital violence characteristics. Additional analysis may reveal that some of the unexplained variation is due to differences in the types of help offered by each help-source. However, it is likely that most of the unexplained variation proceeds from the limitations of the study. A retrospective study based on a single interview, no matter how lengthy, cannot hope to gather enough information on incidents (some of which occurred decades before the time of the interview) to fully explain why certain services received were successful and others were not. With the data at hand, we can do no more than broadly outline the experiences of these battered women and make general comparisons among the various strategies and help-sources employed in the attempt to end the violence.

Intercorrelations among the Success of Formal Help-Sources

The correlation matrix for the wife's use of formal help-sources in the last battering incident is presented in table 6–4. Once again, there are several cells that have too few cases for a correlation coefficient to be calculated. None of the correlations is impressive. The most important observation to be made about table 6–4 is that the observed correlations are negative in every case but one, which indicates that there is a weak, consistent tendency for successfulness in the use of one formal help-source to be associated with lack of success in the use of other formal resources.

The highest correlation relating the success of the use of a help-source in the last and worst incidents is for lawyers and district attorneys (Tau b = .83). Slightly lower levels of consistency of success were found for the police (Tau b = .72) and social-service agencies (Tau b = .73). The consistency of success for women's groups was considerably lower, with a correlation of .54. There were not enough cases in which the clergy were utilized in both the worst and

Table 6–4
Intercorrelations among the Success of Formal Help-Sources in Last Incident

	Police	Social-Service Agencies	Women's Groups	Clergy	Lawyers and D.A.s
Police					
Social-service agencies	−.08				
Women's groups	−.22	−.15			
Clergy	a	−.06	−.24		
Lawyers and D.A.s	.17	−.07	−.17	a	

N = 146; all correlations are Tau b.

[a] Less than 10 cases, or insufficient variation to compute a correlation.

the last incidents to permit the computation of a correlation coefficient. The lower level of the worst-last correlation for the success of women's groups is entirely due to the movement of a handful of ratings from a lack of success in the worst incident to success in the final incident. There were no cases in which the success of a women's group declined from the worst to the last incident.

Comparisons of Formal and Informal Help-Sources

Two of the variables reported in the chapters on formal and informal sources of help may be taken to be indicators of the intensity of help received. These are the mean number of instances of help or sessions per incident and the mean length of the help sequence per incident. Table 6–5 summarizes these variables for shelter services, informal sources of help, and formal sources of help. There is essentially no variability on either dimension for the police, or on the mean number of instances of help for shelter services. For the other variables, the range of values is large, and the means shown are considerably higher than the modes due to the small percentage of incidents in which the level of help provided was of heroic proportions. Among informal sources of help, friends were reported as providing a greater intensity of help to the battered wives than any other source, even the victims' own families. The

Table 6–5
Indicators of the Intensity of Help Received, by Source of Help

Source of Help	Mean Number of Instances of Help or Sessions per Incident [a]	Mean Length of the Help Sequence per Incident [a]
Informal sources of help		
Family	7.2	31 days
In-laws	5.4	34 days
Friends	7.9	84 days
Neighbors	6.4	57 days
Formal sources of help		
Social-services agency	15.5	6.7 months
Lawyer, district attorney	8.1	3.4 months
Clergy	10.7	3.9 months
Police	1.1	1 day[b]
Women's group	19.0	8.5 months
Shelter services	1.0	27 days

N = 146

[a] These statistics are based on the number of incidents in which a source of help became involved, not all incidents.

[b] This statistic is just an estimate in that the mean length of the police help sequence was generally only a matter of minutes.

formal help-source providing the greatest intensity of help was women's groups, followed by social service agencies.

Within each help-source, it is reasonable to assume that the intensity of help increases proportionately with the number of sessions or instances of help per incident and the length of help received per incident. It was hypothesized that the greater the intensity of help received, the more likely the husband would be to react positively (that is to say, by reducing or eliminating the battering) to this intervention. For those instances in which there were at least fifteen cases, the intensity measures were correlated with the husband's reaction for all help-sources utilized in the first, worst, and last battering incidents. The correlations for formal help-sources were generally near zero, and lower than correlations between intensity measures and husband's reaction for help received from family.

It appears that the intensity of help received from informal sources is important to the cessation of the husband's violent behavior, while the intensity of help received from formal help-sources is of doubtful importance. This can be interpreted as meaning that the effect of increasing the intensity of help from family, in-laws, and friends is linear and continuous, while the effect of formal help-source involvement is essentially dichotomous. Any formal help-source involvement at all appears to be about as effective as massive, long-term involvement on behalf of the battered wife. That is to say, if a single visit to a divorce lawyer, from the police, or with a member of the clergy has no effect on the abusive behavior of the aggressor, it is unlikely that multiple visits will be effective.

It may be that the threat of public exposure (and presumably censure) is a powerful deterrent to continued assaults by abusive husbands. If that threat, perhaps reinforced by an initial visit to a formal help-source, is ineffective with a particular husband, the prognosis for ending the battering through repeated visits to (or from) a formal help-source is not good (unless the visits lead to termination of the relationship). This is in direct contrast to the incremental effectiveness of help received from informal help-sources.

We have reported the wives' ratings of the success of various formal and informal help-sources throughout chapters 5 and 6. In addition to the general successfulness of the services received from a help-source, we can also evaluate the helpfulness of services received in terms of the husband's reaction to those services. Table 6–6 displays formal and informal sources of help, as well as the wife's personal efforts to end the battering, rating each of these categories according to their direct impact on the husband's behavior. It is difficult to compare these ratings directly, because the wife's efforts based on her own resources are generally oriented toward the short-term goal of the immediate termination of current violence, while her utilization of informal and formal external sources of help (with the exception of the police) generally occurs between incidents, and is aimed more at long-term

Table 6-6
Violent Husbands' Reactions to Techniques, Strategies, and Sources of Help Utilized by Battered Wives

Strategy, Technique or Source of Help	Husband's Reaction[a]			
	Positive	Neutral	Negative	N^b
Wife's efforts				
Avoidance	34%	19%	46%	448
Hiding	12%	32%	56%	225
Passive defense	1%	1%	98%	782
Talking	31%	42%	28%	283
Promising[c]	54%	46%	0%	392
Threatening	54%	33%	13%	199
Aggressive defense	26%	20%	54%	252
Informal sources of help				
Family	64%	11%	26%	218
In-laws	38%	8%	54%	167
Friends	49%	14%	37%	380
Neighbors	37%	12%	51%	120
Formal sources of help				
Social-service agency	64%	26%	10%	283
Lawyer, district attorney	90%	2%	8%	252
Clergy	49%	27%	24%	132
Police	22%	8%	70%	276
Women's group	54%	33%	13%	197
Shelter services[d]	28%	62%	10%	204

[a] Where percentages do not add up to 100, it is due to statistical rounding procedures. A positive reaction refers to movement toward decreased wife-beating.

[b] This N is the number of instances of use for which data are available. Up to six violent incidents are reported for each subject. Incidents for which husband's or partner's reactions are not known are excluded from the table, as are incidents in which he was unaware of the wife's utilization of a source of help.

[c] Because of the way in which data were collected on the strategy of extracting promises, the proportion of positive outcomes is inflated and is not comparable to the other statistics on positive outcomes.

[d] Provided by both formal and informal sources of help.

than short-term goals. In the Milwaukee study, long-term goal achievement was measured by the general rating of successfulness, and short-term goal achievement was rated by the husband's reaction to the strategy or intervention.

Excluding the husband's reaction to the promising-strategy from the analysis (see chapter 4 for an explanation of the difficulty in interpreting the data on this strategy), it is clear that threatening has the most powerful impact of all the wife's efforts to modify the husband's violent behavior. Attempting to talk the husbands out of the abuse, practicing avoidance, and aggressively defending oneself are considerably less effective. Hiding or passive-defense techniques are extremely ineffective. Among informal sources of help, members of the wife's own family are more likely to have a positive effect on the husband or partner than are friends, with in-laws and neighbors falling behind. The short-term effect of involving lawyers or district attorneys in the abusive situation is positive, and there are also substantial positive effects achieved by the involvement of social-service agencies. Women's groups, the police, the clergy, and shelter services seem to have less positive short-term effects on the aggressors.

These are complex and potentially misleading results. Examination of the qualitative material in the interviews suggests that low-short-term effectiveness as shown in table 6–6 is the product of diametrically opposite processes. In the first process, the aggressor is so threatened by the wife's determination that he often commits negative acts in a last-ditch attempt to maintain control of the relationship through violence. In the second process, the aggressor tends to continue with his pattern of assaultiveness because of the relative impotence or indifference of the help-source. At this point in the analysis, the low effectiveness ratings of the clergy can be characterized as representing relative impotence and the low ratings for the police as indicating indifference. Similarly low positive ratings for women's groups and shelter services appear to be largely a byproduct of the aggressor's final attempt to maintain control. Some evidence in support of this conclusion may also be obtained by comparing the husband's reactions portrayed in table 6–6 with the satisfaction ratings included in the sections on each strategy and help-source.

It is clear from these data that many battered wives actively fight to remove violence from their lives. The efforts to end the abuse suffered by the women in the Milwaukee sample were extensive and intensive, and were completely at variance with the image of the battered women as passively accepting her fate. As the women explored different combinations of strategies and help-sources, they tended to progress from what might be called low-coercion strategies to high-coercion strategies; moving from personal efforts to informal help-sources to formal help-sources. They did not abandon their personal efforts when they added informal and formal help-sources, but integrated these into an armada of forces individualized to be most effective in their own situations.

It is evident from table 6–6 that formal help-sources are more likely to have a significant impact on the husband's battering activities than the wife's efforts on her own behalf. Informal help-sources were close to formal help-sources in short-term effectiveness, but slightly lower in most comparisons. The most potent personal strategy used by the wives, threatening to contact the police or a lawyer, gained at least some of its potency by association with these powerful caretakers of social sanctions. Among the formal help-sources, lawyers and district attorneys had a higher probability of exerting a positive influence on the aggressors than any other help-source.

It is to be expected that the clergy and women's groups would be the least likely to have a positive effect on the battering husbands, but the low ratings for the police appears to be inconsistent with the general hypothesis that increasing severity of social sanctions leads to decreasing battering activity. However, this is the exception that proves the rule, so to speak, for the police made clear in many incidents that they were not willing to support the battered women. There would be little incentive for the husband to reduce or eliminate his spousal assaultiveness if the police communicated their unwillingness to bring social sanctions to bear against him. Furthermore, it may be that the appearance of the police without their imposing social sanctions serves to remove any possible effectiveness from future threats to call the police.

The Husband's Efforts to End the Violence

It would be unfair to pretend that all the efforts to end the bouts of violence were made by the battered wives alone. Some aggressors became sufficiently disturbed by their own behavior to seek help, and others were convinced to do so by their wives. Since interviews were mainly with the victims rather than the aggressors, information about the aggressors' use of help-sources is necessarily more limited than that about the utilization of help-sources by their wives. The accuracy of the reports is probably much higher in the cases of formal sources of help than in the cases of informal sources.

Sixty-nine percent of the subjects reported that their husbands made at least one contact with a formal or informal help-source in an attempt to end the abuse. The average number of help-sources utilized by the aggressors was 4.1. The most common help-source known to the wives was a social-service agency, which accounted for 51 percent of all known help-sources. Self-help groups were involved in 12 percent of the incidents, relatives in 7 percent, and friends in 7 percent. The apparent preponderance of formal help-sources is probably a methodological artifact, since the women were more likely to be aware of their mates' contacting formal help-sources than friends, relatives, or neighbors. The average length of involvement between husbands and help-sources was two and one-half months, during which the modal number of sessions was 8 and the mean number of sessions was 12.9. In one case out of every seven, the length of service was eighteen months or more. The battered wives rated the success of the helping services used by their husbands as very successful in 9 percent of the cases, fairly successful in 47 percent, neither successful nor unsuccessful in 27 percent, fairly unsuccessful in 15 percent, and very unsuccessful in 1 percent.

The most common type of help received by the husbands was focused talking, which comprised 29 percent of the cases. Commanding and directing about problem solving was the next most common type of help received, 23 percent. Other common types of help received were providing material aid or direct service (12 percent), modeling (12 percent), and listening (8 percent). The husbands were sometimes able to get professional counselors to believe that the battering was entirely their spouses' fault or that no battering had occurred, but involvement with Alcoholics Anonymous or other self-help groups brought them into contact with reformed wife-beaters who were impossible to fool.

The importance of the husband's efforts in both ending the violence and improving the marital relationship so that it continued after the end of the abuse should not be minimized. At the same time, the heavy impact of the husband's efforts is not independent of the impact of the wife's own efforts and her involvement of informal and formal help-sources to end the battering. Most of the husbands did not voluntarily seek help. They were pressured into it by their wives, often with help from others. The fact that a husband enters treatment may reflect a change in the marital power balance as much as it does his willingness to receive treatment. Thus, possible success in ending the battering may be due as much to the shift in the power balance as to the actual effects of the treatment itself. It is regretable that the intricacies of the interplay of these factors were not fully captured in our data.

Factors Affecting the Husband's Efforts to End the Violence

Very few of the bivariate correlations between background variables and the husband's efforts to end the violence in the last incident reached ± .15. The strongest of these relationships, between the husband's contacts with his friends and his efforts in the last incident, had a correlation of −.23. This relationship is presented in table 7–1. Husbands who saw their friends daily were less likely to make an effort to end the violence than those who saw friends less often. This may be because the more often husbands saw their friends, the more strongly they were integrated into a peer subculture which legitimated wife-beating. Alternatively, the possibility exists that their friends gave them enough strength to continue to resist their wives' attempts to end their violence. In the only other statistically significant relationships between background variables and the husband's efforts, it was found that husbands high in education and those having a high level of

Table 7–1
Relationship between Frequency of Husband's Contacts with Friends and Husband's Efforts in Last Incident

	Husband's Contacts with Friends	
Husband's Efforts	Less Often Than Daily	Daily
No effort	47%	69%
Some effort	53%	31%
Total	100%	100%
N	45	52

Tau b = −.23

participation in recreational organizations were more likely to make an effort in the last incident than the other former batterers in the sample.

The relationships between various dimensions of marital violence and the husband's efforts produced correlations close to zero in every case except one, which is shown in table 7–2. The more severe the violence in the worst incident, the less likely the husband was to make an effort to end the battering at the time of the last incident.

The husband's efforts in the last incident were unrelated to most of the help-source success ratings. None of the correlations with the success of informal help-sources was far from zero, and the only relationship of any strength involving a formal help-source was with the police. Women who were satisfied with police services were *less* likely to have husbands who made efforts to end the battering in the last incident than women who had unsuccessful police experiences (Tau b = −.25). The success of four of the wives' personal strategies was related to their husbands' efforts. Husbands were more likely to make efforts in families in which the wives were successful with the strategies of promising, threatening, and avoiding violence; but husbands were less likely to make efforts in families in which the wives were successful in hiding. Tables 7–3 and 7–4 document the two most interesting of these relationships.

The consistancy of the husband's efforts between the worst and the last incidents was not as great as the consistancy observed for the wives' personal strategies and the help-sources (Tau b = .35). Exactly half of the husbands made no effort whatever to end the violence in both incidents. Twenty-nine of them made efforts in both incidents, obviously without permanent success after the worst incident. Twenty-eight men who made no effort in the worst incident decided to make an effort in the last incident, but this was partially offset by sixteen men who made an effort in the worst incident and no effort in the last incident.

Table 7–2
Relationship between Most Severe Violence in Worst Incident and Husband's Efforts in Last Incident

Most Severe Violence	Husband's Efforts	
	No Effort	*Some Effort*
Hit, slap, kick, bite, punch	36%	54%
Beat up	39%	30%
Threatened with or used weapons	25%	16%
Total	100%	100%
N	88	57

Tau b = −.17

Table 7–3
Relationship between Wife's Success with Promising and Husband's Efforts in Last Incident

| Husband's Efforts | Success of Promising | | | | |
	Very Un-successful	Fairly Un-successful	Neither	Fairly Successful	Very Successful
No effort	100%	72%	55%	12%	—
Some effort	0%	28%	45%	88%	—
Total	100%	100%	100%	100%	—
N	1	18	38	8	0

Tau b = .32

Table 7–4
Relationship between Wife's Success with Police and Husband's Efforts in Last Incident

| Husband's Efforts | Police Success | | | | |
	Very Un-successful	Fairly Un-successful	Neither	Fairly Successful	Very Successful
No effort	0%	54%	53%	74%	100%
Some effort	100%	46%	47%	26%	0%
Total	100%	100%	100%	100%	100%
N	2	13	15	19	1

Tau b = −.25

The Total Use of Strategies and Help-Sources by the Battered Wives

Chapters 4, 5, and 6 presented material on the wife's use of personal strategies, informal help-sources, and formal help-sources in a series of specific battering incidents. We now look at the total use of these strategies and help-sources by the wives over the entire span of their relationships with their husbands. These dimensions are not merely summaries of the specific incidents examined. They represent the wives' estimates of their total use of these strategies and help-sources for all the battering incidents they experienced.

The most commonly used personal strategy was passive defense. A total of 136 of the battered wives used this strategy, with the modal number of times used being twenty-three. Aggressive defense, threatening, and promising were strategies used by 98 of the battered wives, with the modal number of usages six, four, and nine respectively. Talking was used by 90 of the women, with a modal usage of five times; and the modal usage was seven times among the 82 women who used hiding.

The use of friends as help-sources (109 women, modal usage of eight), and of family members (105 women, modal usage of five) dominated the usage patterns for informal help-sources. Statistics for the other categories of informal help were shelter (87 women, modal usage of four), in-laws (71 women, modal usage of four), and neighbors (54 women, modal usage of four). The total use of informal help-sources is lower than the use of the wife's personal strategies, but it is slightly higher than the use of formal help-sources. The formal help-source usage figures are: social services (108 women, modal usage of four), lawyers or district attorneys (102 women, modal usage of four), police (93 women, modal usage of five), women's groups (81 women, modal usage of three), and clergy (55 women, modal usage of four).

Relationships between Differentiating Variables and the Wife's Total Use of Personal Strategies and Help-Sources

Table 8-1 displays the bivariate correlations between a set of differentiating variables (including demographic characteristics, previous experience with violence, social embedment, and marital characteristics) and the six types of the wife's total use of personal strategies to combat the violence. Avoidance, a seventh strategy, is not included in this part of the analysis because it was

Table 8-1
Relationships between Differentiating Variables and Wife's Total Use of Strategies

Differentiating Variables	Wife's Total Use of Personal Strategies					
	Talk	Promise	Threaten	Hide	Passive Defense	Aggressive Defense
Wife's demographic characteristics						
Mother's occupation	.07	.04	-.10	-.07	-.06	.03
Occupation	.17	.01	.12	.03	.03	-.07
Age	-.06	-.07	.03	.01	-.05	.03
Current marital status	-.06	-.03	-.04	-.02	-.21	-.02
Current income	.08	.00	.21	.08	-.20	-.20
Husband's demographic charcteristics						
Parental income	-.08	.23	.02	.15	-.01	.04
Mother's occupation	.13	-.03	.06	-.02	-.09	.01
Occupation	-.04	-.12	.01	-.03	-.20	-.12
Education	.06	-.08	.07	-.05	-.13	-.14
Armed forces	.06	-.05	.03	-.11	.02	.00
Saw combat	.03	.02	-.12	-.17	-.12	-.07
Joint demographic characteristics						
Year married	.14	.00	-.04	-.05	-.03	-.02
Number of children	.00	.00	.07	.12	.08	.04
Parental income dissimilarity	-.12	-.06	.02	.12	-.03	.03
Occupational dissimilarity	-.12	-.04	.02	-.01	-.10	.03
Previous experience with violence						
Wife assaulted by parents	-.17	-.06	.03	-.06	-.03	.14
Husband assaulted by parents	.09	.13	.02	.09	.16	.03
Premarital violence	.03	.11	.06	.02	.05	.10
Social-embedment variables						
Times moved	.02	.10	.02	-.04	.18	-.03
Wife close to relatives	.17	.11	.00	-.13	.05	-.10
Husband close to relatives	.02	-.01	-.10	.16	.14	.16
Marital characteristics						
Reason for marriage	-.01	-.09	-.09	-.07	-.24	-.08
Problem resolution—recent	-.04	-.03	.07	.00	-.03	.07
Problem resolution—earlier	-.13	-.09	-.05	-.07	.14	.09

N = 146

not originally conceptualized as a specific personal strategy for ending violence.

The scattering of correlations reaching $\pm$ .15 in table 8–1 defies easy summary. The two most influential differentiating variables are current income (directly related to the use of threats and inversely related to the use of passive defense and aggressive defense) and the husband's closeness to his relatives (directly related to the total usage of hiding, passive defense, and aggressive defense). The use of the strategy of passive defense appears to be quite a bit more sensitive to the differentiating variables than any of the other personal strategies. It was most commonly used in those families in which marriage occurred because of pregnancy, where the family moved often, and where the husband was close to his relatives but was assaulted by his parents. Passive defense was also a common strategy where the husband had relatively low occupational status and educational achievement, and where the wife had relatively low current income and did not permanently remain with the batterer after the violence ceased. As the most commonly used strategy, passive defense is highly correlated with the total frequency of beatings experienced by the women. For this reason, these relationships are more reflective of the ecological distribution of total violent incidents than they are of any unique relationship between the differentiating variables and the use of passive defense itself.

There are several trends evident in table 8–2, which indicate that the wife's total use of various informal help-sources is inversely related to her current marital status and also to the educational achievement of her husband. Women who made heavy use of a variety of informal help-sources over the length of the battering relationship were more likely than the other battered women to have married husbands with low educational achievement (and also low occupational status in many cases). They were also more likely to leave their husbands at some time and to eventually seek a permanent separation or a divorce. There is little indication that previous experience with violence, social embedment, or marital characteristics have much of an impact on the wife's total use of informal help-sources.

The most consistant set of relationships in table 8–3 demonstrates the sensitivity of the wife's total use of the police to a variety of indexes of social status. The higher the social status of the wife and the husband, the less frequently the police were utilized as a help-source. A second observation is that the more a woman was forced to utilize (1) the police, (2) social-service agencies, (3) women's groups, and (4) lawyers or district attorneys, the less likely she was to remain married to the batterer. The negative correlations between the occupation of the husband's mother and the use of formal help-sources indicate that wives married to men whose mothers were homemakers were more likely than the other subjects to make heavy use of formal help-sources. Finally, there was a tendency for women who married due to pregnancy to make heavier use of formal help-sources than the other battered wives.

Table 8–2
Relationships between Differentiating Variables and Wife's Total Use of Informal Help-Sources

Differentiating Variables	Wife's Total Use of Informal Help-Sources				
	Family	In-Laws	Neighbors	Friends	Shelter
Wife's demographic characteristics					
Mother's occupation	-.03	-.07	.07	.02	-.07
Occupation	-.09	-.02	-.02	.07	-.05
Age	-.09	-.01	.04	.17	.01
Current marital status	-.21	-.15	.03	-.14	-.37
Current income	-.32	.03	.01	.10	-.06
Husband's demographic charteristics					
Parental income	-.06	.15	.08	-.04	.06
Mother's occupation	-.08	-.01	-.13	-.06	-.17
Occupation	-.25	-.12	-.11	-.11	-.17
Education	-.13	-.21	-.22	-.06	-.17
Armed forces	.02	.03	-.08	-.05	.10
Saw combat	.03	.00	-.12	.03	-.22
Joint demographic characteristics					
Year married	.04	-.06	-.03	-.21	-.07
Number of children	.04	.13	.05	.22	.16
Parental income dissimilarity	.02	.06	.19	.07	.07
Occupational dissimilarity	.00	.02	-.01	.02	.03
Previous experience with violence					
Wife assaulted by parents	.04	.03	-.08	.04	.06
Husband assaulted by parents	.11	.02	.18	.00	.06
Premarital violence	.15	.01	.12	-.18	.04
Social-embedment variables					
Times moved	.08	.18	.09	.07	.14
Wife close to relatives	-.02	-.08	.01	-.07	.04
Husband close to relatives	-.01	-.05	.11	.06	.10
Marital characteristics					
Reason for marriage	-.13	-.01	.05	-.03	.00
Problem resolution—recent	.01	.17	.13	.00	.06
Problem resolution—earlier	-.02	-.13	.03	-.06	-.08

N = 146

Table 8–3
Relationships between Differentiating Variables and Wife's Total Use of Formal Help-Sources

Differentiating Variables	Wife's Total Use of Formal Help-Sources				
	Police	Social Agencies	Women's Groups	Clergy	Lawyers and D.A.s
Wife's demographic characteristics					
Mother's occupation	.01	−.13	−.15	.14	−.06
Occupation	−.17	−.14	−.07	.04	−.11
Age	−.03	−.04	−.10	−.07	−.08
Current marital status	−.22	−.15	−.17	−.06	−.16
Current income	−.19	−.01	−.09	−.23	−.27
Husband's demographic characteristics					
Parental income	−.11	.00	−.16	−.14	.11
Mother's occupation	−.16	−.12	−.22	−.17	−.23
Occupation	−.17	−.10	.00	.15	−.10
Education	−.37	.00	−.04	.02	−.20
Armed forces	.04	.09	.04	.00	.05
Saw combat	−.04	−.26	−.14	−.12	−.08
Joint demographic characteristics					
Year married	−.05	−.01	−.01	−.03	−.01
Number of children	.14	.06	.01	−.01	.12
Parental income dissimilarity	−.02	.02	−.07	−.04	−.02
Occupational dissimilarity	−.05	.05	−.06	−.07	−.05
Previous experience with violence					
Wife assaulted by parents	−.03	−.04	−.15	.02	.07
Husband assaulted by parents	.12	.00	.04	.09	.18
Premarital violence	−.10	.15	.14	.08	.04
Social-embedment variables					
Times moved	.11	.02	.11	.20	.12
Wife close to relatives	.19	.14	−.04	−.09	.00
Husband close to relatives	.01	.17	−.02	.00	−.07
Marital characteristics					
Reason for marriage	−.16	−.19	−.06	−.14	−.10
Problem resolution—recent	−.06	.04	−.05	−.06	−.04
Problem resolution—earlier	.13	.12	−.09	.06	.08

N = 146; all correlations are Tau b

Other Relationships Involving the Wife's Total Use
of Personal Strategies and Help-Sources

As might be expected, there is a direct relationship between the frequency of violent incidents and the total use of various personal strategies and help-sources. Table 8–4 displays these correlations and shows that only talking, threatening, receipt of services from social agencies, and participation in women's groups are essentially unrelated to the total frequency of violence. Of the other marital violence characteristics, violence during pregnancy is predictive of the use of most of the strategies and help-sources, and both the severity of violence and marital rape are predictive of the use of most formal and informal help-sources. The number of years of violence suffered, assaults on children, and the use of chemicals in the worst incident are not generally related to the wife's total use of strategies and help-sources. Neither are the wife's total use of strategies and help-sources generally related to whether or not the husband made an effort to end the abuse in the last incident. Only two of the dimensions of total usage are related to husband's efforts at the ± .15 level or above. These are social services (Tau b = .19) and friends (Tau b = −.15). The women's involvement with Milwaukee social-service agencies appeared to motivate their husbands to make efforts to alter their behavior, while their involvement with friends was negatively associated with husbands' efforts to end the violence.

Analysis of Relationships among the Wife's Total Use
of Strategies and Help-Sources

The correlation matrix for the wife's total use of strategies and help-sources is presented in table 8–5. The intercorrelations in the matrix revolve around the use of the police and lawyers or district attorneys among the formal help-sources; the strategies of promising and passive defense among the wife's own efforts; and the use of in-laws, neighbors, and shelter services among the informal help-sources. The police are clearly the most central factor in the matrix.

These data are organized differently in table 8–6, which presents the rotated factor matrix of a factor analysis of the intercorrelations among the total usage dimensions. Seven factors were produced by the factor analysis procedure. Factor one has high loadings on police, in-laws, neighbors, lawyers, and women's groups. A woman fitting the factor-one profile has little control over her husband. She is unable to influence his behavior through any personal strategies, so she turns to a mixture of those formal and informal help-sources that are most likely to have an impact on her husband. There is also a tendency toward the use of women's groups by

Table 8-4

Relationships between Marital Violence Characteristics and Wife's Total Use of Strategies and Help-Sources

Total Use of Strategies and Help-Sources	Marital Violence Characteristics						
	Frequency	Children Assaulted	Chemicals in Worst Incident	When Pregnant	Marital Rape	Most Severe Violence	Years of Violence
Talk	-.04	.00	-.03	-.02	.01	.02	-.11
Promise	.22	.06	.01	.21	.14	.21	.05
Threaten	.10	.02	.04	.02	-.01	-.04	.10
Hide	.36	.04	.08	.14	.07	.02	.03
Passive defense	.63	.21	.13	.35	.09	.25	.10
Aggressive defense	.20	.10	.08	.13	-.04	-.03	.03
Family	.17	.16	.04	.12	.19	.18	.06
In-laws	.20	-.01	.01	.19	.13	.02	.01
Neighbors	.27	.08	-.03	.15	.16	.15	-.05
Friends	.28	.05	.03	.20	.11	.22	.07
Shelter services	.32	.13	.05	.20	.13	.19	.05
Police	.35	.15	-.07	.25	.27	.20	-.09
Social agencies	.14	.08	-.04	.05	.24	.01	.00
Women's groups	.08	.07	.07	.05	.08	-.15	.06
Clergy	.18	.13	.03	.07	.17	.02	.16
Lawyers and D.A.s	.21	.01	.06	.20	.17	.03	-.03

N = 146; All correlations are Tau b

Table 8–4
Relationships between Marital Violence Characteristics and Wife's Total Use of Strategies and Help-Sources

Total Use of Strategies and Help-Sources		Marital Violence Characteristics					
	Frequency	Children Assaulted	Chemicals in Worst Incident	When Pregnant	Marital Rape	Most Severe Violence	Years of Violence
Talk	-.04	.00	-.03	-.02	.01	.02	-.11
Promise	.22	.06	.01	.21	.14	.21	.05
Threaten	.10	.02	.04	.02	-.01	-.04	.10
Hide	.36	.04	.08	.14	.07	.02	.03
Passive defense	.63	.21	.13	.35	.09	.25	.10
Aggressive defense	.20	.10	.08	.13	-.04	-.03	.03
Family	.17	.16	.04	.12	.19	.18	.06
In-laws	.20	-.01	.01	.19	.13	.02	.01
Neighbors	.27	.08	-.03	.15	.16	.15	-.05
Friends	.28	.05	.03	.20	.11	.22	.07
Shelter services	.32	.13	.05	.20	.13	.19	.05
Police	.35	.15	-.07	.25	.27	.20	-.09
Social agencies	.14	.08	-.04	.05	.24	.01	.00
Women's groups	.08	.07	.07	.05	.08	-.15	.06
Clergy	.18	.13	.03	.07	.17	.02	.16
Lawyers and D.A.s	.21	.01	.06	.20	.17	.03	-.03

N = 146; All correlations are Tau b

Table 8–6
Factor Analysis of Wife's Total Use of Strategies and Help-Sources

Total Use of Strategies and Help-Sources	Factor 1	Factor 2	Factor 3	Factor 4	Factor 5	Factor 6	Factor 7
Rotated factor matrix							
Talk	-.063	.000	-.043	-.043	-.020	-.063	.274
Promise	.280	.254	-.197	.018	.326	-.007	.084
Threaten	.041	.063	.040	-.521	-.022	.011	-.002
Hide	.167	.125	.112	-.072	-.066	-.084	-.099
Passive defense	.131	.484	.098	.162	.075	.046	.364
Aggressive defense	.045	.126	.747	.006	.013	.067	-.013
Family	.081	.131	.052	.042	.618	.066	.021
In-laws	.505	.130	-.030	-.072	.040	.015	-.092
Neighbors	.497	-.050	.141	.266	.128	.074	.398
Friends	.125	.145	.076	.158	.141	.010	.253
Shelter services	.114	.592	.079	.042	.310	.031	-.109
Police	.517	.367	.147	.412	.152	.088	-.183
Social-service agencies	.130	.003	.056	-.023	.083	.688	-.085
Women's groups	.363	-.012	-.007	-.039	.060	.152	-.074
Clergy	.107	.211	-.251	.167	-.174	.249	.026
Lawyers and D.A.s	.399	.204	.025	.304	.004	.290	-.108

N = 146

factor-one women. We can venture a guess that factor-one marriages are very unsatisfactory for the wives, and we would expect them to want to terminate many of these relationships at some time.

Factor two has high loadings on passive defense, the police, and shelter services. Women fitting the factor-two profile are thoroughly dominated by their husbands and rely mainly on the police or on escaping from the situation to prevent further battering. Factor three has a high loading on only aggressive defense. The factor-three profile portrays a woman who fights back directly against her abusive husband and may be able to, in a sense, beat him at his own game. Factor four has a high positive loading on the police and a high negative loading on threatening. A woman fitting the factor-four profile would depend heavily upon the formal help offered by the police and also to some extent on lawyers, but would be unlikely to threaten to call them in an attempt to control her husband. For such a woman, threats might not be effective because they would tend to provoke an escalation of violence rather than control the aggression.

Factor five, with its very high loading on the use of family members and its lower loadings on the use of the strategy of promising and shelter services, leads us to believe that women fitting this profile would have fairly good relationships with their husbands and would be strongly embedded in the social system. Factor six consists almost entirely of formal help-sources, but unlike factor one, the highest loading is on social-service agencies, and the loadings on informal help-sources are close to zero. The final factor has the highest loadings on neighbors and passive defense, with other moderately high loadings on talking and the use of friends. Women fitting the profile of factor seven would be similar to those in factor five in that they would be unwilling to involve external authorities in their private affairs. In addition, they would depend on help-sources that would not confront their husbands. These women might have enough confidence in their marital relationships to feel comfortable talking them out of continued abuse. Reviewing the seven factors, it is interesting that the only factor dominated by use of the wife's own strategies is factor three, which has a heavy loading on aggressive defense. Apparently, less direct defenses that do not confront the husband are not adequate in themselves to achieve success in ending the battering. They must be combined with the use of help-sources from outside of the marital dyad.

9

What Works Best Overall: The Cessation of Violence

This chapter focuses on the wife's judgment of her most and least successful efforts in ending the battering in the last incident, as well as her global judgments about how the abuse ceased, her specific recommendations and general advice to other battered women based on her own experiences. Since the women in the study have managed to end the battering, their opinions of what works are invaluable and should be made known to women who are currently being abused.

What Worked Best and Least in Ending the Battering in the Last Incident

It is evident in table 9-1 that no single strategy or help-source was the most effective element in ending the battering in the last incident for more than twenty-one of the women. The most common element cited was talking to friends, which occurred in 14 percent of the cases. Other common elements were threats (12 percent), aggressively defending oneself (10 percent), contacting a women's group (10 percent), contacting a social-service agency (9 percent), taking shelter (8 percent), and talking to family members (7 percent). Formal help-sources were as likely to be cited as informal help-sources, and the wife's personal strategies are not far behind.

There is no simple pattern in these data. Rather, women in different situations clearly found different factors to be most effective in ending the battering. No one solution or even a group of related solutions to the problem of wife-battering arose on this intimate level, to say nothing of more general social-policy levels.

These generalizations are upheld in table 9-2, which presents data on what worked least in ending the abuse in the last incident. Once again, no single factor or related group of factors predominates. However, there is a clear tendency for informal help-sources to be less often cited as the least successful factors in ending the battering than either the wife's strategies or formal help-sources. The factors most likely to be labelled as least successful are the promising-strategy (14 percent), calling the police (11 percent), contacting a lawyer or district attorney (8 percent), trying to talk the husband out of further abuse (7 percent), contacting a social-service agency (5 percent), and aggressively defending oneself (5 percent).

Table 9-1
What Worked Best in Ending Battering in Last Incident?

Factors	Number of Cases	Percentage
Talk husband out of abuse	5	3
Threats (nonviolent)	17	12
Hiding	4	3
Passively defending self	1	1
Aggressively defending self	15	10
Talking to own relatives	10	7
Talking to in-laws·	4	3
Talking to neighbors	5	3
Talking to friends	21	14
Talking to anyone else	4	3
Taking shelter	11	8
Calling the police	7	5
Contacting a social-service agency	13	9
Contacting a women's group	15	10
Contacting the clergy	4	3
Contacting a lawyer or D.A.	7	5
Other	2	2
Nothing	1	1
Total	146	102[a]

[a] Percentages do not sum 100 due to rounding.

Table 9-2
What Worked Least in Ending Battering in Last Incident?

Factors	Number of Cases	Percentage
Talk husband out of abuse	10	7
Get husband to promise cessation	21	14
Threats (nonviolent)	4	3
Hiding	3	2
Passively defending self	1	1
Aggressively defending self	7	5
Talking to own relatives	4	3
Talking to in-laws	6	4
Talking to neighbors	1	1
Talking to friends	2	1
Talking to anyone else	1	1
Calling the police	16	11
Contacting a social-service agency	7	5
Contacting a women's group	1	1
Contacting the clergy	4	3
Contacting a lawyer or D.A.	11	8
Nothing	46	32
Total	145	102[a]

[a] Percentages do not sum 100 due to rounding.

The Cessation Experience

Tables 9-3 and 9-4 look at cessation as a general process rather than as related to any specific battering incident. Table 9-3 displays the battered wives' answers to questions about the factors enabling them to demand an

Table 9–3
What Enabled Wife to Force Husband to End Battering?

Factors	Number of Cases	Percentage
Fear for self	19	13
Fear for children	7	5
Had enough, decided had to act	40	28
Family members gave confidence	18	13
Women's groups gave confidence and information	33	23
Social service agencies gave confidence and aid	18	13
Other	6	4
Total	141	99[a]

[a] Percentages do not sum 100 due to rounding.

Table 9–4
What Enabled or Forced Husband to End Battering?

Factors	Number of Cases	Percentage
Accepted changes in his wife	9	10
Wanted to reestablish their relationship	23	25
Feared divorce	27	30
Feared police or criminal legal action	19	21
Other	13	14
Total	91	100

end to the violence. Two factors were mentioned much more often than any others. The first was that 27 percent of the women had simply had enough and decided that the abuse must end. The second factor, which was mentioned by 23 percent of the women, was that their participation in women's groups gave them the confidence and information necessary to end the battering. The importance of the social support of women's groups as a force to end marital violence is clearly shown by this factor. Other factors commonly cited by the women included (1) that their fear for their own safety drove them to end the battering, (2) that their contact with members of their own families gave them the confidence necessary to do the job, and (3) that their experiences with social-service agencies allowed them to develop the personal confidence and gave them the direct aid necessary to end the violence.

Opinions of the battered wives indicated that the most important factor in their husbands' willingness to end the battering was fear of divorce. This was mentioned by 30 percent of the women. Twenty-five percent of the men had a more positive motivation, in that they wished to reestablish a healthy relationship with their wives and realized that the battering was fundamental to the process that forced them apart over the years. Two other common factors influencing the husbands to end the battering were fear of the police or of criminal legal action, and acceptance of attitudinal and behavioral changes in the wives that rendered abusive measures futile in maintaining dominance. The factors reported to be associated with positive action to end the abuse contrast strikingly for the husbands and wives. For the wives, it was a matter of personal growth, gaining personal strength, and increasing their reality-testing ability. On the other hand, the men were slightly more likely to be motivated to end the battering by fear of some sort of action by the police or the courts than by more positive factors. It was more common for husbands to respond to ultimatums to end the abuse than to willingly alter their behavior.

Some women developed a combination of personal strategies and help-sources that seemed to have promise, and they consistently followed this pattern, wearing down their husbands in the process until they finally gave up beating them. Other women did not find success until they hit upon a new combination or added a new source of help. This changed their situation at home in a matter of weeks or a few months, leaving them suddenly violence-free. Here are a few of these success stories.

Sharon had, over the years, blamed herself for the beatings. She tried to keep away from Herman as much as possible when he was in bad moods, thus avoiding many beatings. Begging Herman to refrain from beating her had no effect on his violence. She occasionally stayed with friends or relatives overnight as part of her avoidance strategy. What changed her life was a weekend spent with a church friend who convinced her that she was a fine wife and Herman was completely wrong. Her friend helped her realize that Herman's violence could not be justified by anything Sharon did because violence was contrary to the message of love that Christ brought to humankind. Armed with a radically different view of herself and their marriage, Sharon confronted Herman and used the religious arguments learned from her friend to force Herman to see himself as sinful. As a religious man, Herman was taken aback by Sharon's arguments as well as her new strength and determination. He agreed to join her in counseling with their minister and to seek a renewed life in Christ.

Isabel called the police every time the batterings became severe. She sometimes had sympathetic officers, sometimes not. On those occasions when they indicated she could press charges she always refused, afraid of upsetting her husband still further. Her life changed the day she was feeling particularly spunky and filed assault charges with the district attorney. Although she did not continue the case to trial, filing charges was sufficient to convince her husband that he would end up in jail if he didn't treat her with more respect.

Karen was in her fifties, her children were now on their own, and she was still a battered wife. After two decades of escape, avoidance, and denial, she decided to tell everything to her married daughter, who had always been her husband's favorite child. Her daughter was shocked and concerned when she heard the details of what she had only vaguely suspected.

She arranged to have an entire evening alone with her father. Without revealing how much she knew about his violence, she convinced him to start attending Alcoholics Anonymous by agreeing to go with him to the weekly meetings. It was through AA that he began to realize how much of a drinking problem he had and how his abuse of alcohol was linked to his abuse of his wife. The problem came out in the open at an AA meeting six months later, when he stood up and told the entire story to the group. Karen was never beaten after that night.

Recommendations and Advice to Currently Battered Wives

Having triumphed over their own victimization, the Milwaukee women were in a position to make specific recommendations to other battered wives and to give them general advice about what would be likely to work best in ending the battering. Table 9–5 displays the specific recommendations made by the battered wives based on their own experiences. These recommendations are skewed toward formal help-sources, with contacting a social-service agency (24 percent) and contacting a women's group (23 percent) accounting for nearly half of the recommendations. Other common recommendations include taking shelter, contacting a lawyer or district attorney, and talking to friends about the problem.

The general advice given by our subjects to other battered women (table 9–6) is more consistent with their reports of what ultimately enabled them to end the battering. The most common piece of advice refers to internal states rather than external conditions: "Don't let the pattern persist, no matter

Table 9–5
Wife's Recommendations to Others, Based on Own Experiences

Factors	Number of Cases	Percentage
Talk husband out of abuse	2	1
Threaten husband	6	4
Hide	1	1
Aggressively defend self	4	3
Talk to relatives	5	4
Talk to in-laws	4	3
Talk to friends	11	8
Talk to anyone else	1	1
Take shelter	17	12
Call police	3	2
Contact social-service agency	34	24
Contact women's group	33	23
Contact the clergy	2	1
Contact a lawyer or D.A.	14	10
Other	6	4
Total	143	101[a]

[a] Percentages do not sum 100 due to rounding.

Table 9–6
Wife's General Advice to Other Battered Women

Factors	Number of Cases	Percentage
Tell anyone you can trust about the problem	16	11
Don't let the pattern persist, no matter what	42	29
Seek the aid of a professional counselor	38	26
Leave the batterer	36	25
Press charges against the batterer	8	6
Other	4	3
Total	144	100

what." Twenty-nine percent of the subjects relayed this as the primary piece of general advice. The second most commonlymentioned general advice was to seek the aid of a professional counselor (26 percent), and the third was to leave the batterer (25 percent). The only other elements of general advice to be mentioned by more than one subject were: "Tell anyone you can trust about the problem," and "Press charges against the batterer." It is noteworthy that this general advice pushes currently battered wives to quickly become involved with as many powerful sources of help as possible. Successful women do not recommend trying endless personal strategies or keeping the violence a secret to avoid embarrassment in the community. They also do not recommend that you plan to stay with your husband if the batterings continue.

The strong character of these women comes through in their general advice to other battered women. At one time, most felt weak in dealing with their husbands, but that is no longer the case. Faced with a problem that seemed insurmountable and, in most cases, went on for many years, they triumphed over it. In doing so, they developed an inner strength that also aided them in making other changes in their lives. In the following comments, some of these women speak for themselves.

> Don't tolerate abuse. When you say stop it, mean it. Leave the situation if it gets close to violence. Recognize that you don't need to be dependent. Put yourself as number one. Don't assume blame for the abuse.

> Rely on friends and family members who will help you. Don't be afraid to reach out to find help. Seek refuge away from your husband when he becomes violent. Don't say anything unless you can back it up.

> Figure out what your husband is most proud of and threaten that. Threatening to call the police and telling hospital staff how you got those bruises are effective. Avoid arguments that aren't going anywhere. Set up an escape plan in case violence erupts. It may be possible to set up a signal with neighbors so they can call the police.

Both husband and wife need to be able to walk away from an argument that is getting out of hand. Each must be respectful of the other during discussions and must be willing to compromise.

When first you're hit, give your husband a year. If he hasn't quit by then leave him. Use a friend or a professional counselor to help you sort out the situation. Explore all alternatives.

Don't keep it inside. Talk with people about the violence, even if they do no more than listen. The more people know, the easier it is to shame your husband into quitting the violence. Don't be too proud to rely on help from your family.

Try marriage counseling if your husband is willing. If not, try to find another third party to offer insight. The next step is to shop around for legal help. Female lawyers and counselors are better than their male counterparts.

Call the police the first time it happens. Press charges to stop the beatings. If you don't, the abuse gets worse. Try to get your husband into counseling so he can work on his jealously, anger, and lack of respect for women. He may need to overcome his insecurities.

Counselors are only good if they've been battered themselves. The clergy don't know what violence and domination are all about. Press charges and work through the legal system. The judge can slap a restraining order on your husband while you are waiting for the trial.

Get help as early as possible. Don't give up. Some couples aren't meant to stay together, but at least give it a try. Don't push an irrational man, especially if he drinks. Find out all about you legal rights before you do anything drastic.

Don't be sarcastic with the police when they come. Play the cop game so they don't become threatened. You'll get better service.

Crisis hotlines are great.

Shelters are fine for you and the kids, but they don't help your husband change. He needs counseling and treatment. Try to get him into therapy or a group for battered men.

Nip violence in the bud. Don't fool yourself into believing that a bad situation will get better by itself. The abuser doesn't really see the problem, no matter how much he apologizes and promises to change. Don't get married if there is any hint of violence in the relationship.

Learn all you can about your husband before you get married. Pay attention to your own gut reactions. Never let your husband know that using violence will get him his way. Once that happens, he'll beat you every time he wants to win an argument or influence a family decision.

Keep everything on the record—at the hospital, with the district attorney, lawyer, and police. Always call the police when attacked. Make lots of noise so the neighbors will know. Try to accumulate some money on the side so you will be able to leave when you've had enough.

Variables Effecting the Cessation Experience

Having failed to demonstrate any outstanding patterns between background variables and violence characteristics on the one hand, and the success of various strategies and help-sources on the other hand, we might expect few strong relationships in the analysis of the cessation variables. That is unfortunately the case, and the data displayed in tables 9–7 through 9–10 allow us to make only a small number of generalizations about these relationships. Once again, the sociological variables used in the study are not able to explain more than a small proportion of the variation in the cessation experiences of the battered wives. In the bivariate analyses of the cessation experience, the categories were ordered from the wife's personal strategies through informal help-sources to formal help-sources. Thus the correlations are between various independent variables and the degree of formality (or social-sanctioning ability) of the strategies and help-sources found to be successful in ending the violence.

In table 9–7, an assortment of background variables are cross-tabulated with what worked best and least in ending the battering in the last incident. Older women, those who stayed married to their husbands, and those with higher current incomes were more likely to find personal strategies or informal help-sources best in ending abuse in the last incident. Variables low in formality were also most effective with husbands having middle-or upper-class background, who had never been assaulted by their parents, and who did not dominate the decision-making process in the marriages. Paradoxically, women who remained in their marriages and who had lower current incomes were also more likely to cite variables low in formality as those least effective in ending the battering in the last incident. This may be interpreted as meaning that the same group of women made heavy use of personal strategies and informal help-sources, some of them finding these strategies most successful, and others finding them least successful in ending abuse in the last incident.

The only four background factors in table 9–8 that relate to more than a single cessation variable are wife's age, husband's parental income, current marital status, and year of marriage. Older women were more likely to favor personal strategies and informal help-sources for their recommendations and general advice, as well as for their estimates of what influenced their husbands to end the abuse. On the other hand, women who had been married for a long period of time were more likely than other battered women to give high ratings to formal help-sources. In the third factor, women who elected to remain married to their husbands were more likely to

Table 9–7
Relationships between Differentiating Variables and
What Worked in Ending Last Incident

Differentiating	What Worked?	
Variables	Best	Least
Wife's demographic characteristics		
Mother's occupation	.00	−.02
Occupation	.01	.13
Age	−.13	−.08
Current marital status	−.16	−.34
Current income	−.12	−.21
Husband's demographic characteristics		
Parental income	−.29	−.16
Mother's occupation	−.04	−.14
Occupation	.03	−.02
Education	−.04	.00
Armed forces	.05	.00
Saw combat	−.11	−.18
Joint demographic characteristics		
Year married	.02	.00
Number of children	.05	.01
Parental income dissimilarity	.07	.04
Occupational dissimilarity	−.02	−.09
Previous experience with violence		
Wife assaulted by parents	.08	.12
Husband assaulted by parents	.13	.00
Premarital violence	.05	−.01
Social-embedment variables		
Times moved	.04	−.02
Wife close to relatives	−.07	.01
Husband close to relatives	.09	.11
Marital characteristics		
Reason for marriage	−.03	−.03
Problem resolution—recent	.07	−.08
Problem resolution—earlier	.20	.09

N=146; all correlations are Tau b

mention personal strategies or informal help-sources as significant in ending the violence. Finally, women whose husbands came from families that were relatively well-off financially were more likely than other subjects to cite formal help-sources as influencing both their own and their husbands' behavior toward ending the abuse.

The characteristics of the violence suffered by the battered women apparently have almost nothing to do with what works best or least in ending abuse. Only one of fourteen correlations presented in table 9–9 is above ±.15. Involvement of chemicals in the worst incident is associated with lack of success in the use of resources high in formal-sanctioning ability. In table 9–10, we find that women raped by their husbands were more likely than the other battered women to mention formal help-sources as what enabled them

Table 9-8

Relationships between Differentiating and Cessation Variables

	Cessation Variables			
Differentiating Variables	Wife's Enablers	Husband's Enablers	Wife's Recommendations	Wife's General Advice
Wife's demographic characteristics				
Mother's occupation	-.09	.04	.13	.00
Occupation	-.10	-.04	-.10	.04
Age	-.01	-.25	-.18	-.14
Current marital status	-.10	-.29	.00	-.16
Current income	.03	-.03	.03	-.04
Husband's demographic characteristics				
Parental income	.20	.23	.10	.02
Mother's occupation	.03	-.11	-.10	.02
Occupation	.05	-.05	-.10	.05
Education	-.14	-.05	.00	-.03
Armed forces	.00	-.01	-.08	-.08
Saw combat	-.02	.09	.06	.02
Joint demographic characteristics				
Year married	-.05	.28	.15	.06
Number of children	.02	-.11	-.01	-.05
Parental income dissimilarity	-.03	.11	.11	.12
Occupational dissimilarity	.11	.03	.08	-.01
Previous experience with violence				
Wife assaulted by parents	.00	-.04	.02	-.04
Husband assaulted by parents	-.09	.14	.17	.08
Premarital violence	-.05	.08	-.01	-.02
Social-embedment variables				
Times moved	.06	-.06	.05	.10
Wife close to relatives	.10	.05	.00	.02
Husband close to relatives	.09	-.01	.11	.06
Marital characteristics				
Reason for marriage	.05	-.04	.05	-.01
Problem resolution—recent	.01	-.03	.01	-.06
Problem resolution—earlier	.03	-.06	.02	.05

N=146; all correlations are Tau b

Table 9-9

Relationships between Marital Violence Characteristics and What Worked in Ending Last Incident

	What Worked?	
Marital-Violence Characteristics	Best	Least
Frequency	.12	.14
Children assaulted	.04	.12
Chemicals in worst incident	-.01	-.19
When pregnant	-.02	.15
Marital rape	.12	.12
Most severe violence	.02	-.06
Years of violence	-.04	.06

N = 146; all correlations are Tau b

Table 9–10
Relationships between Marital Violence Characteristics
and Cessation Variables

Differentiating Variables	Cessation Variables			
	Wife's Enablers	Husband's Enablers	Wife's Recommendations	Wife's General Advice
Frequency	.10	.10	.00	.09
Children assaulted	.08	.03	−.01	.06
Chemicals in worst incident	.06	−.08	.07	−.10
When pregnant	.03	−.15	−.05	.14
Marital rape	.19	.08	.03	.12
Most severe violence	.03	.07	−.01	.14
Years of violence	.04	−.31	−.16	−.03

N = 146; all correlations are Tau b

to demand and obtain an end to the violence. The longer the total period of violence, the more likely women were to recommend the use of personal strategies or informal help-sources to other battered wives and to see these low-formality factors as important in motivating their husbands to end the violence. Women who were beaten while pregnant were also more likely than the other women to see low-formality factors as significant in their husbands' decision to end the violence in their marriages.

Perhaps the best way to summarize these results is to say that almost any strategy or help-source can ultimately work. The crucial factor is not always the nature of the strategy or help-source; what really matters is the woman's showing her determination that the violence *must stop now*. Once the batterers in the Milwaukee study became convinced of their wives' determination to end the violence, they usually reassessed their position in the marriage and decided to reform. Of course, this is only true for those husbands who value their marriages and wish to continue them.

10 Integration with Previous Research and Recommendations

This chapter consists of two parts. In the first part, the Milwaukee findings are integrated with a selection of the outstanding studies in the field around four points of discussion. The second part consists of recommendations about ways to decrease the incidence of marital violence in U.S. society.

Integration with Previous Research

Scientific knowledge develops through the constant interplay of theory and data, existing literature and new studies, and the arguments of proponents of competing theories for the explanation of similar phenomena. The following sections relate the Milwaukee data to outstanding earlier studies that collected data on learned helplessness, marital power, social embedment, and the use and evaluation of personal strategies and help-sources.

Learned Helplessness

In her book, *The Battered Woman* [66], Lenore Walker observed that repeated beatings produce passivity in abused wives. Feeling helpless to stop the beatings, the battered wives generalize the helplessness until it permeates every aspect of their lives. They develop negative self-images and expect to fail at everything they try to do. This is one reason why many battered women stay with their abusers for so many years.

In interviewing only women who had overcome abuse, the Milwaukee researchers recruited a different sample of women than those interviewed by Walker. At the time they were interviewed, these women hardly exemplified the learned-helplessness syndrome. Quite to the contrary, most of the previously battered women had developed active mastery over their lives, not only with respect to the battering, but also in many divergent areas of importance to them. It is true that learned helplessness was present in most of these women early in their relationships with their husbands. However, in triumphing over the battering the women also reduced or eliminated their feelings of helplessness. In short, they exhibited learned competence instead of learned helplessness.

Walker believes that the first step in ending learned helplessness is to persuade the battered women (or the batterer) to leave the relationship. This is consistent with the Milwaukee finding of a high number of separations that occurred during the years when the women in the sample were gaining the necessary strength to demand an end to the battering. It is also possible to agree that " . . . battered women need to be taught to change their failure expectancy to reverse a negative cognitive set" [66:53]. The Milwaukee data show that this can be successfully accomplished through informal contacts, generally with friends and family members, and through participation in women's groups. While it is true that "counseling or psychotherapy can teach women to control their own lives and to be able to erase that kind of victim potential" [66:54], professional therapists were not as successful as women's groups in helping the Milwaukee battered women overcome the effects of learned helplessness.

Marital Power

Frieze [30] and Adler [47] have both presented data that link marital violence to the marital power struggle. Although these data are hardly conclusive, they are consistant with the thesis that a major reason for the use of marital violence is to increase one's power over a mate. This was true in the majority of the families participating in the Milwaukee study. Male domination of marital decision-making processes was not limited to decisions about where to take a vacation and which appliances to buy. For many of the women, it meant total control over every aspect of their lives, including their relationships with friends and even with their own children.

The cessation of violence was associated with decreased male dominance in many of the relationships. Unfortunately, the nature of the study precluded collecting information on minute changes in the marital power balance that occurred after each battering incident, so it is not possible to comment on these micro-level phenomena.

Social Embedment

In a recent unpublished paper, Donato [143] surveyed the existing literature relating social embedment to the length of the battering relationship. She found that, in general, high social-embedment was associated with longer periods of marital violence. This undermines the assumption that social control operates through social embedment (as well as through other mechanisms) to reduce criminal behavior, including wife-beating. The literature on social embedment appears to provide some support for the theory of societal patriarchial control advanced by Dobash and Dobash [2]. It may be true, as Straus et al. [82] suggests, that a marriage license is a hitting license. The Milwaukee data are remarkable for the low association between social-embedment variables and the characteristics of marital violence among the battered women. The families of the most severely battered women were no more or less socially embedded than families of the least severely battered women. These data offer confirmation for neither the traditional theory of social embedment nor the feminist patriarchal theory of social embedment.

The single exception to this is the consistent positive relationship between the frequency of the husband's contact with his friends and the seriousness of the marital violence. Contacts with friends were associated with high frequency of battering, assaults on children, the use of chemicals (predominantly alcohol), beatings when wife was pregnant, and the severity of violence. These correlations, when combined with a number of other relationships, suggest a theoretical interpretation not anticipated in the development of the study, and therefore only sketchily covered in the interviews. According to this theory, battering husbands have developed standards of gratification that demand that they completely dominate their wives and children. When this domination is threatened, they feel deprived, suffer psychic distress, and react with a rage that appears to be uncontrollable, but is actually contrived to reestablish the domination patterns that meet their standards of gratification. The idea of standards of gratification as being a causal determinant in social problems is not new. It was first proposed in the early 1960s by Harry Bredemier. Standards of gratification are not innate. They are learned through the perception of environmental stimuli, and they vary in strength directly with the support received from the social environment.

Many batterers begin to develop standards of gratification demanding domestic dominance when they see their mothers dominated by their fathers and experience this domination themselves as children in their families of orientation. The idea that maleness demands domination is further supported by many of the patriarchial ideas that have general circulation in U.S. society. It is certainly possible for standards of gratification developed during childhood to persist throughout adult life with the assistance of general cultural elements of patriarchal dominance. But the fullest development of such standards that lead to marital violence occurs in those men who are heavily immersed in social relationships with male peers who constantly reinforce these standards of gratification-through-dominance. There is no national lobby that favors wife-beating. However, the myriad peer-relationships that support the patriarchal dominance of the family and the use of violence to enforce it may constitute a subculture of violence. The more fully a husband is immersed in this subculture, the more likely he is to batter his wife.

This is not a subculture that is confined to a single social class, religion, occupational grouping, or race. It is spread throughout all parts of society. Men are socialized by other subculture members to accept common definitions of the situation, norms, values, and beliefs about male dominance and the necessity of keeping their wives in line. These violence-supporting social relations may occur at any time and in any place. For most subculture participants they probably center around work, involvement in informal participatory sports activities, and socializing in bars and similar gathering places. Because the Milwaukee study did not directly deal with the idea of a male subculture of violence, one can only guess at its broad outlines. Research involving males who batter their wives is necessary to test the hypothesis of the relationship between a male patriarchal subculture and wife-beating, for most of the interaction in the subculture is not viewed by the battered wives.

Use and Evaluation of Help-Sources

Three of the studies providing data on the utilization and evaluation of informal and formal help-sources were carried out by Frieze et al. [32], Schulman [89], and Pagelow [27]. Frieze found that the wife's own relatives were more likely to be sought out for help in connection with battering than any other help-source. They were approached by 55 percent of the women, as compared with 52 percent who sought out friends, 43 percent who contacted social-service agencies, 42 percent who approached therapists, and 39 percent who sought out priests. The average helpfulness of the various help-sources showed almost no variation. Nearly two-thirds of the women (who were recruited from shelters and court records, and via posted advertisements) contacted the police in connection with one or more battering incidents. They were as likely to feel that the police caused further harm in their situations with the batterers as they were to feel that the police were helpful. Just over half of the women had filed legal charges at some time during their relationships with their husbands.

Schulman used a random sample of Kentucky women to identify a smaller group of battered wives who were presumably representative of all Kentucky battered wives. They were much more satisfied by their experiences with the police than were the battered wives studied by Frieze et al. Sixty-four percent of the Kentucky women expressed satisfaction with police services, and only 34 percent expressed dissatisfaction. Few of the women had utilized battered-women's shelters, but one-quarter of them would like to have had formal shelter services available to them. The most common person with whom they discussed the incident was a family member (61 percent), or a friend (49 percent). The clergy (14 percent) and agency workers or therapists (19 percent) were much less likely to be sought out for help in connection with the battering.

The responses of Pagelow's sample of women from battered women's-shelters illustrate the low average-quality of service delivered by police officers to battered wives. Only 32 percent of the officers summoned by the battered wives displayed positive attitudes toward them. Fifty-five percent of the women contacted the police, as compared with 44 percent who contacted lawyers or other legal agents, 28 percent who contacted psychiatrists or psychologists, 22 percent who contacted the clergy, and 15 percent who contacted marriage counselors. The women generally found legal professionals and marriage counselors to be more helpful than psychiatrists, psychologists, and the clergy.

Frieze et al., Schulman, and Pagelow did not make effectiveness of help-sources the major focus of their studies. They therefore did not have as much detail on these help-source dimensions as was gathered in the Milwaukee study. The broad outline of their findings is consistant with the pattern found in the Milwaukee data. The major differences are that Frieze et al. found little variation in the helpfulness of formal and informal help-sources, and that Schulman found a surprisingly high level of satisfaction with the police. The major points of similarity are (1) the low ratings of the police given in two of the three studies, (2) the great excess of need for shelter services (and other supportive services) over available services implied in the Kentucky study, (3) the heavy use of the police and the legal profession by battered women, (4) the higher use of informal help-sources (friends and relatives) than formal help-sources, (5) the relatively low use of the clergy as a help-source, and (6) Pagelow's ranking of the legal profession and marriage counseling as being more effective than the clergy. It is not possible to comment on her findings that marriage counselors are more helpful than psychiatrists or psychologists, as the Milwaukee study did not break down social-service agencies in this way.

Recommendations

1. Currently battered women need to receive advice about the wealth of personal strategies informal help-sources, and formal help-sources that they can use in ending their victimization. Information should be provided through all possible avenues, including the media, social-service agencies, battered-women's organizations, and lawyers' offices. In addition, this information should be made available in places such as supermarkets, welfare offices, and shopping malls so that women who may not yet have become battered wives or for whom the battering may just be beginning can prepare to defend themselves and to keep the pattern of abuse from becoming established in their families. There is also a need to continually reevaluate and refine the data on personal strategies and help-sources that have been produced in the Milwaukee study.

2. The heavy use of sheltering by the battered women in the study implies that the need for sheltering services is even greater than has previously been estimated by the supporters of battered-women's shelters. An obvious recommendation is that additional public funds should be diverted to open new battered-women's shelters. In addition, there should be a guarantee of continuing, full support for existing shelters. It is clear that there will not be enough shelters to meet the needs of the battered women in southeastern Wisconsin, even if many new facilities are opened. The state should consider providing financial support for private citizens who are giving shelter to battered women and their children through informal helping-networks, as this is the only way to meet the needs of battered women who cannot be cared for through formal shelter organizations. The technical problems involved in such reimbursement are considerable, but the program is not beyond the realm of possibility. Pamphlets intended to help battered women deal with their husbands can also be designed for use by members of informal helping-networks offering support.

3. The very high success ratings given by the battered wives to women's groups suggests that it would be efficient for agency and general public funds to be diverted to increase the level of support for these groups. They can often be efficiently combined with shelter services under multipurpose agencies. Where a women's group is developed within an existing agency, it should be kept independent of the agency's bureaucratic structure and its treatment-modality preferences as much as possible. The Milwaukee findings tell us that the individuals who are responsible for the operation of these groups (and who are often indigenous paraprofessionals rather than fully accredited professional therapists) are remarkably capable of delivering effective services to battered wives. Rather than weakening these services by making them conform to traditional service-delivery models, existing agencies should look carefully at the treatment models used by women's groups to determine what elements of these models can be incorporated into their own service-delivery systems.

4. With the exception of women's groups, a significant proportion of all of the individuals in helping agencies and criminal-justice organizations are in need of training about the nature of family violence, the needs of battered women, and the personal strategies and help-sources that are effective in combating marital violence. The use of indigenous paraprofessionals (once-battered women who can serve as role models and deliver other services to currently-battered wives) as staff members should be encouraged.

5. The rather dismal ratings given to help received from police officers suggests that the services provided to battered women by police departments should be targeted by public-interest groups as needing an immediate upgrading. Officers should receive additional training in the handling of domestic disputes so that they can better meet the needs of the complainants

in these cases within the framework of the law. In addition, they should routinely and uniformly inform all battered women or potentially battered women of their legal rights and should also distribute pamphlets referring them to other appropriate help-sources.

6. To the extent that husbands who batter are supported in their marital violence by their participation in a male peer subculture of violence, it will not be easy to treat them using individualistic models of service delivery. If they are heavily enmeshed in this peer subculture, they will need to change their friends in order to sustain any gains that are made in treatment. Self-help groups built on the model of Alcoholics Anonymous may be the most successful behavior-change modality for these individuals. Batterers who do not have this level of peer-group support can be expected to be more amenable to individual therapy, marital therapy, and standard group-therapy techniques.

References

1. Goode, William J. "Force and Violence in the Family." *Journal of Marriage and the Family* 33 (1971):624–636.

2. Dobash, R.E., and Dobash, R.P. *Violence Against Wives: A Case Against the Patriarchy.* New York: Free Press, 1979.

3. Martin, Del. *Battered Wives.* San Francisco: Glide Publications, 1976.

4.———. "Scope of the Problem." In *Battered Women: Issues of Public Policy.* Washington, D.C.: U.S. Commission on Civil Rights, 1978, pp. 205–227.

5. Dobash, R.E., and Dobash, R.P. "Wife Beating—Still a Common Form of Violence." *Social Work Today,* 15 November 1977, pp. 14–18.

6. ———."Wives: The 'Appropriate' Victims of Marital Violence," *Victimology* 2 (1978):426–442.

7. Mawby, R.I. "A Note on Domestic Disputes Reported to the Police." *Howard Journal of Penology and Crime Prevention* 17 (1978): 160–168.

8. Van Fossen, Beth E. "Intersexual Violence in Monroe County, New York." *Victimology* 4 (1979):299–304.

9. Maryland Commission for Women. "Maryland Battered Spouse Report." Mimeographed. Baltimore, MD, 1979.

10. Zagaria, Pam. "Battered Women: the Hidden Problem." St. Paul, MN: Board of Directors of the Community Planning Organization, Inc., 1976.

11. Anderson, Gordon A; Sweet, Richard; and Lythcott, Stephen. "Information on Domestic Violence in Wisconsin: Extent and Services Available." *Research Bulletin 78–2.* Madison: Wisconsin Legislative Council, 1978.

12. Bard, Morton, and Zacker, Joseph. "Assaultiveness and Alcohol Use in Family Disputes—Police Perceptions." *Criminology* 12 (1974): 281–292.

13. Milwaukee Task Force on Battered Women. "Domestic Violence—Fact Sheet." Mimeographed. Milwaukee, 1977.

14. Whitehurst, Robert N. "Violence Potential in Extra–Marital Sexual Responses." *Journal of Marriage and the Family* 33 (1971):683–691.

15. O'Brien, John E. "Violence in Divorce–Prone Families." *Journal of Marriage and the Family* 33 (1971):692–698.

16. Levinger, George. "Source of Marital Satisfaction Among Applicants for Divorce." *American Journal of Orthopsychiatry* 36 (1966): 804–806.

17. Parker, Barbara, and Schumacher, Dale N. "The Battered Wife Syndrome and Violence in the Nuclear Family of Origin: A Controlled Pilot Study." *American Journal of Public Health* 67 (1977):760–761.

18. Fields, Marjory D. "Wife Beating: Government Intervention Policies and Procedures" In *Battered Women: Issues of Public Policy*. Washington, D.C.: U.S. Commission on Civil Rights, 1978, pp. 228–287.

19. Pfouts, Jane H. "Violent Families, Coping Responses of Abused Wives." *Child Welfare* 57 (1978):101–111.

20. Ball, Margaret. "Issues of Violence in Family Casework." *Social Casework* 58 (1977):3–12.

21. Gayford, J.J. "Battered Wives." *Medical Science and the Law* 15 (1975):237–245.

22. ———. "Wife Battering: A Preliminary Survey of 100 Cases." *British Medical Journal* 1 (1975):194–197.

23. ———. "The Aetiology of Repeated Serious Assaults by Husbands on Wives (Wife Battering)." *Medicine, Science and the Law* 19 (1979):19–24.

24. Carlson, Bonnie E. "Battered Women and Their Assailants." *Social Work* 22 (1977):455–460.

25. Rounsaville, Bruce J. "Theories in Marital Violence: Evidence from a Study of Battered Women." *Victimology* 3 (1978):11–31.

26. Pagelow, Mildred D. "Secondary Battering: Breaking the Cycle of Domestic Violence." Paper presented at the annual meeting of the Sociologists for Women in Society, Chicago, 1977.

27. ———.*Woman Battering: Victims of Spouse Abuse and Their Perceptions of Violent Relationships*, Ph.D. dissertation, University of California, Riverside, 1980.

28. Ferraro, Kathleen J. "Definitional Problems in Wife Battering." Paper presented at the annual meeting of the Pacific Sociological Association, Anaheim, 1979.

29. ———. "Physical vs. Emotional Battering: A Study of Responsibility." Paper presented at the annual meeting of the Pacific Sociological Association, Anaheim, 1979.

30. Frieze, Irene H. "Power and Influence in Violent and Nonviolent Marriages." Paper presented at the annual meeting of the Eastern Psychological Association, Philadelphia, 1979.

31. ———. "Causal Attributions as Mediators of Battered Women's Responses to Battering." Part of the Final Report of Grant #1 R01 MH 30193 to the National Institute of Mental Health, 1980.

32. Frieze, Irene H.; Knoble, Jaime; Washburn, Carol; and Zomnir,

Gretchen. "Characteristics of Battered Women and Their Marriages." Part of the Final Report of Grant #1 R01 MH30193 to the National Institute of Mental Health, 1980.

33. Browne, Stephen F. "'In Sickness and In Health . . . ': Analysis of a Battered Women Population." Denver: Denver Anti–Crime Council, 1980.

34. McNeely, R.L., and Jones, Joan M. "A Haven from Abuse: Objectives and Organization of Services at the Sojourner Truth House for Battered Women." Unpublished manuscript. Milwaukee: University of Wisconsin–Milwaukee, 1980.

35. Reynolds, Lynn. "Wife Abuse: The Issue is Power," Paper presented at the annual meeting of the American Sociological Association, New York, 1980.

36. URSA Institute. "Domestic Violence Programs, National Analysis." Mimeographed draft. San Francisco, 1980.

37. Vaughan, Sharon R. "The Last Refuge: Shelter for Battered Women." *Victimology* 4 (1978):113–119.

38. LaBell, Linda S. "A Sociological Study of Battered Women and Their Mates." *Victimology* 4 (1979):258–267.

39. Korlath, Maureen J. "Alcoholism in Battered Women: A Report of Advocacy Services to Clients in a Detoxification Famility." *Victimology* 4 (1979):292–298.

40. Star, Barbara. "Comparing Battered and Non-Battered Women." *Victimology* 3 (1978):32–44.

41. Dobash, R. Emerson. "Violence Against Wives: Some Research Notes." *Scottish Branch Social Services Research Group Newsletter*, no. 5 (1978), pp. 24–28.

42. Dobash, R. Emerson; Dobash, D.P.; Cavanagh, C.; and Wilson, M. "Victimology Interviews: Wife Beating: The Victims Speak." *Victimology* 2 (1978):608–622.

43. Ashley, Martha S. "Shelters: Short-Term Needs," In *Battered Women: Issues of Public Policy*. Washington, D.C.: U.S. Commission on Civil Rights, 1978.

44. Spezeski, Pat, and Warner, Carmen G. *Spouse Assault*. San Diego: County Department of Human Services, 1977.

45. Back, Susan M., et al. *A Monograph on Services to Battered Women*. Washington, D.C.: Government Printing Office, 1980.

46. Roberts, Albert R. *Sheltering Battered Women: A National Survey and Service Guide*. New York: Springer, 1981.

47. Adler, Emily S. "The Underside of Married Life: Power, Influence and Violence" In *Women and Crime in America*, edited by Lee H. Bowker, pp. 300–320. New York: Macmillan, 1981.

48. Straus, Murray A. "Leveling, Civility and Violence in the Family." *Journal of Marriage and the Family* 36 (1974):13–30.

49. Allen, Craig M., and Straus, Murray A. "Resources, Power and Husband-Wife Violence," In *The Social Causes of Husband–Wife Violence*, edited by Murray A. Straus and Gerald T. Hotaling. Minneapolis: University of Minnesota Press, 1979.

50. Kinsey, Alfred C.; Pomeroy, Wardell B.; Martin, Clyde E.; and Gebbard, Paul H. *Sexual Behavior in the Human Female*. Philadelphia: W.B. Saunders, 1953.

51. Hite, Shere. *The Hite Report*. New York: Macmillan, 1976.

52. Bartell, Gilbert D. *Group Sex*. New York: Peter H. Wyden, 1971.

53. Wolff, Charlotte. *Love Between Women*. New York: Harper and Row, 1971.

54. Califia, Pat. "Lesbian Sexuality." *Journal of Homosexuality* 4 (1979):255–266.

55. Gelles, Richard J. *The Violent Home*. Beverly Hills: Sage Publications, 1974.

56. ———. "Violence and Pregnancy: A Note on the Extent of the Problems and Needed Services." *The Family Coordinator* 24 (1975):81–86.

57. Gelles, Richard J. "Abused Wives: Why Do They Stay?" *Journal of Marriage and the Family* 38 (1976):659–668.

58. ———. *Family Violence*. Beverly Hills, CA: Sage, 1979.

59. Marsden, Dennis, and Owens, David. "The Jekyll and Hyde Marriages." *New Society* 32 (1975):333–335.

60. Whitehurst, Robert N. "Male Violence: Rules and Rationalizations." Paper presented at the annual meeting of the American Sociological Association, Boston, 1979.

61. Billings, Andrew G.; Kessler, Marc; Gomberg, Christopher A.; and Weiner, Sheldon. "Marital Conflict Resolution of Alcohol and Nonalcoholic Couples during Drinking and Nondrinking Sessions." *Journal of Studies on Alcohol* 40 (1979):183–195.

62. Adrian, Martha, and Mitchell, Carol. *A Study of Spouse Battering in Montana*. Helena: Department of Community Affairs, State of Montana, 1978.

63. Doran, Julie B. "Conflict and Violence in Intimate Relationships: Focus on Marital Rape." Paper presented at the annual meeting of the American Sociological Association, New York, 1980.

64. Frieze, Irene H.; McCreanor, Marylynn; and Shomo, Kathy. "Male Views of the Violent Marriage," Paper presented at the annual meeting of the Association for Women in Psychology, Santa Monica, CA, 1980.

65. Walker, Lenore E. "Treatment Alternatives for Battered Women," In *The Victimization of Women*, edited by Jane P. Roberts and Margaret Gates. Beverly Hills: Sage Publications, 1978, pp. 143–174.

66. ———. *The Battered Woman*. New York: Harper and Row, 1979.

67. ———. "How Battering Happens and How to Stop It." In *Battered Women*, edited by Donna M. Moore, Beverly Hills, CA: Sage, 1979.

68. Nielsen, Joyce M.; Eberle, Patricia; Thoennes, Nancy; and Walker, Lenore. "Why Women Stay in Battering Relationships: Preliminary Results," Paper presented at the annual meeting of the American Sociological Association, Boston, 1979.

69. Steinmetz, Suzanne K. *The Cycle of Violence: Assertive, Aggressive and Abusive Family Interaction*. New York: Praeger Publishers, 1977.

70. ———. "The Use of Force for Resolving Family Conflict: The Training Ground for Abuse." *The Family Coordinator* 26 (1977):19–26.

71. ———. "Wifebeating, Husbandbeating—A Comparison of the Use of Physical Violence Between Spouses to Resolve Marital Fights." in M. Roy, *Battered Women: A Psychosociological Study of Domestic Violence*, New York: Van Nostrand Reinhold, 1977, pp. 63–72.

72. ———. "The Battered Husband Syndrome." *Victimology* 2 (1978):499–509.

73. Yllo, Kersti, and Straus, Murray A. "Interpersonal Violence Among Married and Cohabiting Couples." Paper presented at the annual meeting of the National Council on Family Relations, 1978.

74. Cazenave, Noel A., and Straus, Murray A. "Race, Class, Network Embeddedness and Family Violence: A search for Potent Support Systems." *Journal of Comparative Family Studies* 10 (1979):280–299.

75. Coleman, Diane H., and Straus, Murray A. "Alcohol Abuse and Family Violence." Paper presented at the annual meeting of the American Sociological Association, Boston, 1979.

76. Dibble, Ursula G., and Straus, Murray A. "Some Social Structural Determinants of Attitudes and Behavior with Respect to Domestic Violence." *Journal of Marriage and the Family* 42 (1980):71–80.

77. Straus, Murray A. "A Sociological Perspective on the Prevention and Treatment of Wifebeating," In *Battered Women: A Psychological Study of Domestic Violence*, edited by M. Roy. New York: Van Nostrand Reinhold, 1977, pp. 194–239.

78. ———. "National Survey of Domestic Violence: Some Preliminary Findings and Implications for Future Research." Prepared for hearings on Research Into Domestic Violence, U.S. House of Representatives, Committee on Science and Technology, 14 February, 1978.

79. ———. "Wife Beating: How Common and Why?" *Victimology* 2 (1978):443–458.

80. ———. "Measuring Intrafamily Conflict and Violence: The Con-

flict Tactics (CT) Scales" *Journal of Marriage and the Family* 41 (1979): 75–88.

81. ———. "Family Patterns Associated with Child Abuse in a Nationally Representative American Sample," *Child Abuse and Neglect* 3 (1979):213–225.

82. Straus, Murray A.; Gelles, Richard; and Steinmetz, Suzanne. *Behind Closed Doors: Violence in the American Family*. Garden City, NY: Doubleday, 1980.

83. Gelles, Richard J., and Straus, Murray A. "Violence in the American Family." *Journal of Social Issues* 35 (1979):15–39.

84. Gaquin, Deirdre A. "Spouse Abuse: Data from the National Crime Survey." *Victimology* 2 (1978):632–643.

85. Saltzman, Linda E., and Featherston, Fran. "Domestic Assault: An Examination of National Crime Survey Respondents," Paper presented at the annual meeting of the American Society of Criminology, San Francisco, 1980.

86. Nisonoff, Linda, and Bitman, Irving. "Spouse Abuse: Incidence and Relationship to Selected Demographic Variables." *Victimology* 4 (1978): 131–140.

87. Ulbrich, Patricia, and Huber, Joan "The effect of Observing Parental Violence on Gender-Role Attitudes." Paper presented at the annual meeting of the American Sociological Association, Boston, 1979.

88. Stachura, James S., and Teske, Raymond H.C., Jr. *A Special Report on Spouse Abuse in Texas*. Huntsville, TX: Criminal Justice Center, Sam Houston State University, 1979.

89. Schulman, Mark A. *A Survey of Spousal Violence Against Women in Kentucky*. Lexington: Kentucky Commission on Women, 1979.

90. Dobash, R. Emerson. "The Relationship Between Violence Directed at Women and Violence Directed at Children Within the Family Setting." House of Commons, Parliamentary Select Committee on Violence in the Family, 1977.

91. Moore, Jean G. "Yo–Yo Children—Victims of Matrimonial Violence." *Child Welfare* 54 (1975):557–566.

92. Roy, Maria. "A Current Survey of 150 Cases," In *Battered Women: A Psychosociological Study of Domestic Violence*. Edited by M. Roy pp. 25–44. New York: Van Nostrand Reinhold, 1977.

93. Straus, Murray A. "Cultural and Social Organizational Influences on Violence Between Family Members." In *Configurations: Biological and Cultural Factors in Sexuality and Family Life*, edited by R. Prince and D. Barrier, pp. 53–69. Lexington, D.C. Heath, 1974.

94. Patterson, Gerald R. "The Aggressive Child: Victim and Architect of a Coercive System," In *Behavior Modification and Families*, edited by E.J. Mash; L.A. Hamerlynck; and L.C. Handy, pp. 267–316. New York: Brunner/Mazel, 1976.

95. Paterson, Eva J. "How the Legal System Responds to Battered Women," In *Battered Women*, edited by Donna M. Moore. Beverly Hills, CA: Sage, 1979.

96. Parmas, Raymond. "Police Discretion and Diversion of Incidents of Intra-Family Violence." *Law and Contemporary Problems* 36 (1971): 539–565.

97. Eisenberg, Sue E., and Micklow, Patricia L. "The Assaulted Wife: 'Catch 22' Revisited." *Women's Rights Law Reporter* 3 (1977): 138–161.

98. Bard, Morton. "Family Intervention Police Teams as a Community Mental Health Resource." *Journal of Criminal Law, Criminology and Police Science* 60 (1969):247–250.

99. Langley, Roger, and Levy, Richard C. "Wife Abuse and the Police Response." *FBI Law Enforcement Bulletin* 47 (1978):5–9.

100. Frederick, Robert E. *Domestic Violence: A Guide for Police Response,* Harrisburg: Pennsylvania Coalition Against Domestic Violence, 1979.

101. Bard, Morton, and Zacker, Joseph. "The Prevention of Family Violence: Dilemmas of Community Intervention." *Journal of Marriage and the Family* 33 (1971):677–682.

102. Bard, Morton, and Connolly, Harriet. "The Police and Family Violence: Policy and Practice" In *Battered Women: Issues of Public Policy*, U.S. Commission on Civil Rights. Washington, D.C.: 1978, pp. 304–326.

103. Flynn, John P. "Recent Findings Related to Wife Abuse." *Social Casework* 58 (1977):13–20.

104. Oppenlander, Nancy. "Coping or Copping Out: Police Service Delivery in Domestic Arguments and Assaults." Paper presented at the annual meeting of the American Society of Criminology, San Francisco, 1980.

105. Haffner, Sarah. "A Refuge for Battered Women." *Victimology* 4 (1979):100–112.

106. Klein, Dorie. "Can This Marriage be Saved?: Battery and Sheltering." *Crime and Social Justice* 12 (1979):19–33.

107. Bell, Joseph N. "Rescuing the Battered Wife." *Human Behavior* 6 (1977):16–23.

108. Center for Women Policy Studies. *Programs Providing Services to Battered Women*. Washington, D.C.: Government Printing Office, 1980.

109. Ferraro, Kathleen J. "Hard Love: Letting Go of an Abusive Husband." Paper presented at the annual meeting of the Society for the Study of Social Problems, San Francisco, 1978.

110. Marcovitch, Anne. "Refuges for Battered Women." *Social Work Today* 7 (1976):34–35.

111. Lowenberg, David A. "Conjugal Assaults: The Incarcerated or Liberated Woman." *Federal Probation* 41 (1977):10–13.

112. Bowker, Lee H. "A Scream in the Night: Women as Victims." In *Women, Crime and the Criminal Justice System*, edited by Lee H. Bowker, pp. 103–142. Lexington, Mass.: D.C. Heath and Company 1978.

113. Pagelow, Mildred D. "Secondary Battering: Alternatives of Female Victims to Domestic Violence." In *Women and Crime in America*, edited by Lee H. Bowker, pp. 277–300 New York: Macmillan, 1981.

114. Scott, P.D. "Battered Wives." *British Journal of Psychiatry* 124 (1974):433–441.

115. O'Neil, Michael J. "A Little Help From Our Friends: Citizen Predisposition to Intervene in Spouse Abuse." *Law and Policy Quarterly* 1 (1979):177–206.

116. O'Farrell, Timothy. "Marital Stability Among Wives of Alcoholics: Reported Antecedents of a Wife's Decision to Separate from or Endure Her Alcoholic Husband." Ph.D. dissertation, Boston University, 1975.

117. Silverman, Phyllis R. *Mutual Help Groups: A Guide for Mental Health Workers*. Washington, D.C.: Government Printing Office, 1978.

118. President's Commission on Mental Health. *Report to the President, Volume II, Task Panel Reports*. Washington, D.C.: Government Printing Office, 1978.

119. Gartner, Alan, and Riessman, F. *Self-Help in the Human Services*. San Francisco: Jossey–Bass, 1977.

120. Gartner, Alan. "Self-Help and Mental Health," *Social Policy* 7 (1976):28–40.

121. Powell, T. "The Use of Self-Help Groups as Supportive Reference Communities." *American Journal of Orthopsychiatry* 45 (1975): 756–764.

122. Reissman, Frank. "How Does Self-Help Work?" *Social Policy* 7 (1976):41–45.

123. Levy, L.H. "Self-Help Groups: Types and Psychological Processes." *Journal of Applied Behavioral Science* 12 (1976):310–322.

124. Katz, A.H. "Self-Help Organizations and Volunteer Participation in Social Welfare." *Social Work* 15 (1970):51–60.

125. Durman, Eugene C. "The Role of Self-Help in Service Provision." *Journal of Applied Behavioral Science* 12 (1976):433–443.

126. Henderson, S. "The Social Network, Support and Neurosis: The Function of Attachment in Adult Life." *British Journal of Psychiatry* 131 (1977):185–191.

127. Miller, P.M., and Ingham J.G. "Friends, Confidants and Symptoms." *Social Psychiatry* 11 (1976):51–58.

128. Cobb, S. "Social Support as a Moderator of Life Stress." *Psychosomatic Medicine* 38 (1976):300–314.

129. Gottlieb, Benjamin H. "The Development and Application of a Classification Scheme of Informal Helping Behaviors." *Canadian Journal of Behavioral Science* 10 (1978):105–115.

130. Reeder, Sharon. "The Influence of Social Networks on the Use of Health Services." Paper presented at the annual meeting of the American Sociological Association, Boston, 1979.

131. Hahn, Susan L.; Moore, Margaret J.; and Stark, Tamra L. *White Paper on Self-Care*. Milwaukee, WI: Consumer Health Consultants, 1979.

132. Ladinsky, Jack; Macaulay, Stuart; and Anderson, Jill. *The Milwaukee Dispute Mapping Project: A Preliminary Report*. Working Paper 1979–3 of the Disputes Processing Research Program. Madison: University of Wisconsin Law School, 1979.

133. Ladinsky, Jack and Susmilch, Charles. "The Processing of Consumer Disputes in a Metropolitan Setting." Paper presented at the annual meeting of the Midwest Political Science Association, Chicago, 1980.

134. Tolsdorf, C.C. "Social Networks, Support and Coping: An Exploratory Study." *Family Process* 15 (1976):407–417.

135. Collins, A.H. "Natural Delivery Systems: Accessible Sources of Power for Mental Health." *American Journal of Orthopsychiatry* 43 (1973): 46–52.

136. Finlayson, A. "Social Networks as Coping Resources: Lay Help and Consultation Patterns Used by Women in Husbands' Post Infarction Career." *Social Science and Medicine* 10 (1976):97–103.

137. Cannon–Bonventre, Kristina and Kahn, Janet R. *The Ecology of Help-Seeking Behavior Among Adolescent Parents*. Cambridge, MA: American Insitutes for Research, 1979.

138. Lieberman, Morton A. and Bond, Gary R. "The Problem of Being a Woman: A Survey of 1,700 Women in Consciousness–Raising Groups," *Journal of Applied Behavioral Science* 12 (1976):363–379.

139. McKinlay, J.B. "Social Networks, Lay Consultation and Help-Seeking Behavior." *Social Forces* 51 (1973):275–292.

140. McShane, Claudette and Oliver, John. "Women's Groups as Alternative Human Service Agenices." *Journal of Sociology and Social Welfare* 5 (1978):615–626.

141. Crowley, C.J.; Jordan, J.; Iperen, L. Van; and Vennard, P. *Physically Abused Women and Their Families: The Need for Community Services*. Trenton: New Jersey Dept. of Human Services, 1978.

142. Wahler, Robert G. "The Insular Mother: Her Problems in Parent-Child Treatment." Unpublished paper. University of Tennessee, 1978.

143. Donato, Katharine. "Battered Women and Social Embeddedness: A Literature Review." Unpublished paper. Milwaukee University of Wisconsin–Milwaukee, 1981.

Index

About the Author

Lee H. Bowker is the dean of the Graduate School and Research at Indiana University of Pennsylvania. He is the author of *Prisoner Subcultures* (Lexington Books, 1977); *Women, Crime, and the Criminal Justice System* (Lexington Books, 1978); *Humanizing Institutions for the Aged* (Lexington Books, 1982); *Women and Crime in America*; *Prison Victimization*; and *Corrections: The Science and the Art*. He has also published articles in such journals as *Crime and Delinquency*, *International Journal of Women's Studies*, *Adolescence*, *Victimology*, *The International Journal of Comparative and Applied Criminal Justice*, the *United Nations Bulletin on Narcotics*, and *Liberal Education*. His current interests are in the structure of academic disciplines, behavior and administration in institutions, sex roles and sexual oppression, and geriatric service-delivery systems.